Advance praise for *Closing the Assessment "Loop"*

Myers demystifies the assessment process with this helpful book. While acknowledging the difficulty of thorough assessment, he assures the reader that the task is not impossible and argues convincingly that it is essential if institutions are to succeed in achieving their mission. In Myers's view, assessment is intentional, systemic, ongoing, and missional as opposed to being either punitive or perfunctory. This perspective allows him to connect the theory and practice of assessment to the practical demands of the accreditation process without making accreditation the focus of assessment. Myers deserves kudos for helping to make the assessment process clear for theological educators (and institutions) who often fear the word and question its value for theological schools.

Edward L. Wheeler, President, Christian Theological Seminary

This book, like Bill Myers, is pragmatic and easily accessible. It will serve as a useful resource for theological schools as they prepare self-study reports for accrediting purposes, and as they engage in regular and ongoing assessment processes.

Marsha Foster Boyd, Director of Accreditation and Leadership Education,
The Association of Theological Schools in the United States and Canada

Not to fear, this introduction to the process of assessment in theological schools is inviting. Simply stated, assessment is interpretation—seeking to understand the mission to which we are called and the faithfulness of our response. Thanks to Bill Myers, faculty, administrators, and board members are invited to gather together in a process designed to help them make informed and strategic choices for their school.

Jack L. Seymour, Academic Dean, Garrett-Evangelical Theological Seminary

Bill's postscript, in an automotive analogy, commends attention to the system and its parts. While there isn't a comparable assessment system you can drive off the lot, Bill's book provides a thoughtful, experience-based guide to the two alternatives: build it yourself from scratch or "some assembly required." Old hands and neophytes, alike, will benefit from this work.

Louis Charles Willard, Director, Accreditation and Institutional Evaluation,
The Association of Theological Schools in the United States and Canada

Closing the
Assessment "Loop"

Closing the Assessment "Loop"

Nurturing Healthy, On-going Self-evaluation in Theological Schools

WILLIAM R. MYERS

Exploration Press
Chicago, Illinois

Publisher:

Exploration Press

Chicago Theological Seminary

5757 S. University Avenue

Chicago, Illinois 60637

Library of Congress Cataloging-in-Publication Data

Closing the Assessment "Loop":
Nurturing Healthy, On-going Self-Evaluatin in Theological Schools
by William R. Myers

ISBN-13: 978-0-913552-70-4

ISBN-10: 0-913552-70-4

Book and cover design by Bob Barker

Printed in the United States of America.

For my parents,
Margaret E. and William A. Myers

TABLE OF CONTENTS

Acknowledgments

While I am responsible for the reflections, both the helpful ones and those that may not be so helpful, that are found in this book, I did not come to them on my own. Whatever insights I offer came my way while I served as Academic Dean at Chicago Theological Seminary and in my present position as Director of Leadership Education and Accreditation at The Association of Theological Schools in the United States and Canada (ATS). Initial drafts of this manuscript were produced under the ever helpful and steady hands of Fran Pacienza and Nancy Merrill, and of Scott Haldeman, my editor. Chapters were re-worked after numerous workshops and critical comments from helpful friends, including George Brown, Jeremiah McCarthy, Marsha Foster Boyd, Charles Willard, Daniel Aleshire, and Doug Lewis. My thanks to them and to the staff at ATS. Without Barbara Kimes Myers, however, I would never have written this book. For her, thanks hardly suffices.

Administrators, faculty members and trustees in theological schools find the word "assessment" passing their lips and ringing in their ears regularly these days. It is a word that often raises anxieties and sometimes provokes anger. For many, the anxiety is connected to the accreditation process. Administrators recognize that when their schools are visited by accreditation evaluation committees, they can expect to be found wanting in the area of assessment. Anger can arise at this point because accreditation agencies seem to revel in jargon-laden requirements that are not easily understood or accomplished by theological educators. This perception is made stronger when accreditation visitors seemingly assume that assessment is good only when it produces hard data (i.e., numbers) that can be easily graded.

In response, officers of theological schools argue that such practices are more appropriate to the measurement of annual corn productivity or the tensile strength of rolled steel than to the relational discernment required in aiding adults in their development as pastoral leaders, scholars and the like. In addition, the lock-step approach to assessment as applied by some overzealous visitors only provides theologians with an easy target. When the approach is wooden, theologians readily condemn the entire enterprise as a belabored effort to unseat God. Such assessment processes, they proclaim, leave little or no room for God's grace that surprisingly abounds in the education of ministers. Such criticisms, whether completely accurate or not, should give accrediting agencies pause.

At the same time, most administrators in theological schools readily admit that their own practices could stand some improvement, practices that in many cases are related to the concerns presumably addressed by that peculiar word, "assessment." Further, they also admit their belated recognition that assessment is after all, only a word, and that this word might prove to be useful were it to refer to and involve the employment of evaluative practices appropriate to theological education. They may even, when pressed, confess that good stewardship of the educational institutions entrusted to them mandates a second look at assessment in light of their knowledge of some older words, words like discernment, witnessing, and truth-telling.

To develop and articulate an approach to assessment that is appropriate to the contexts of theological education is the intent of this book.

William R. Myers
Pittsburgh, Pennsylvania
Summer 2005

1

CHAPTER 1

A FOUR-STEP PROCESS OF ASSESSMENT

"It is a capital mistake to theorize before one has data."

Sir Arthur Conan Doyle[1]

Jeff Goldblum's character in *The Big Chill* reminds his friends that rationalization is more important than sex, when he asks: "Have you ever gone a week without a rationalization?" Whether or not you agree with his criterion, we must admit that the same is true of assessment. We use assessment procedures every day. For example, whether we are considering the purchase of a car, a pair of shoes, or a new t-shirt, assessment procedures are in play. Larger concerns also give rise to the practice of assessment: "What school are you going to attend? Is this the right job for me?" In daily living, people can be said to engage in such decision-making on the basis of **four steps** that constitute an assessment process, the same sort of process accrediting agencies are asking theological schools to develop and employ.

The initial assessment step has to do with raising a concern or a possibility related to the discrepancy between "is" and what "ought to be" and which takes the form of thoughtful **questioning**. Consider, for example, what happens when there is water in the basement of a house following every rainstorm.

The homeowners, quite reasonably, are convinced of two things: that the home should not have water in the basement and that in the long run such a recurring issue will adversely affect the house. So, they ask themselves the question: "The basement wall at the front of our house is leaking after every rainstorm. What should we do?" Note that there is a prior "standard" in play here: a "good" home does not have a leaky basement.

Such questioning pushes the homeowner to identify persons and procedures that might address the problem or deficiency. The homeowner actively collects good **data**, embarking on assessment step number two.

The homeowner talks to the owner of a hardware store and quickly discovers an "expert" who can use a backhoe to dig out the dirt and "seal" the wall for $800. A second friend notes that hanging a "good gutter" where the roof overlaps the basement wall might solve the problem for $200 or less. A family member suggests that using a cheap plastic shield while reconfiguring the landscaping near the wall might redirect water from the wall to the front lawn. He suggests a cost of $100 or less.

The gathered data then need to be sifted through and discussed by those who live in the house (and who will pay the bills and live with the results).

A third assessment step, therefore, has to do with the **screening and interpretation of the collected data.** What do these data mean?

> After an extensive conversation among homeowners and several extended family members, the cost of the backhoe operator's solution seems to be out of the question at this particular moment; other impinging bills push this "solution" into the future. Careful consideration by all gathered of the available remaining data seem to find both the gutter and the water diversion options viable, both because of their logic in addressing the issue and because both could be cheaply done by members of the extended family.

No more data will be sought; the homeowners move to step four.

Assessment step four has to do with **considering strategic alternatives, choosing one, and, then, implementing this option.** Strategy and tactics enter the process.

> Given their financial situation and the possibility of success for less than $100, the homeowners decide to go (first) with the cheapest strategy; that is, the re-contoured drainage area. They invite extended family members to a "Saturday workday" and begin to purchase the necessary materials to make such a day successful. When the work was completed on that day, one person remarked, "It just might work." Another suggested, "And you'll know one way or another after the next hard rain."

Looking at this series of events as an assessment process, one might note that this cycle is open-ended. If the reconfiguration of the drainage area solves the issue, all will rejoice. If not, a gutter will be hung. If this also fails, then the backhoe operator/cellar sealer will be contracted for the job (of course, after due diligence is done with bids requested from several other construction companies). Assessment, even in this wet basement example, is an ongoing, overlapping process.

The assessment process in a theological school

Schools have three areas where assessment must occur: (1) student learning assessment, (2) department, or "unit" assessment, including academic degree program assessment, and (3) overall institutional assessment.

Theological educators know that there are standard educational practices that accrediting agencies expect to find in place in each of these areas. They also expect that accreditors will look at how the school seeks on-going improvement within each area. In student learning assessment, the focus is on how and what the students learn. In academic degree program assessment, the focus is each academic degree offered by the school. Ongoing institutional assessment involves regularized, administrative assessment of the president, administrators, faculty, and staff; the various institutional offices, such as the admissions office, development office, business office, the academic program, and buildings and grounds; and the ways such assessment comes together to shape the overall strategic plan of the institution in terms of resources, mission, constituency, context, and the like.

Accreditors approach each of these areas with a basic idea of what should be in place in order to meet their agency's criteria. In other words, they assume a school's assessment plan will have identified all the basement leaks and will have thought through potential strategies that might address these issues and/or move the school to a new (and better) level of performance.

While different tools and procedures might be used for each area of assessment, the process of assessment always moves from a prior recognition of a standard to include the four named steps:
questioning;
data gathering;
interpretation; and
strategic choosing/tactical implementation of an option.

The Four Steps

For example, a first constructive assessment step in a theological school involves the **posing of good questions.** In other words, within each department, office, assessment team, or council, certain questions should emerge about specific issues or the standards agreed upon as "good practice" for which this group has responsibility. Such issues often arise in departmental meetings or in a "task force" committee. For example, as a result of focused conversation on specific topics, concerns about student housing are voiced. While it appears that no specific accrediting standard applies, comments about there being too many empty rooms and low morale among the residents are directed from staff members in the student services office to the President's Council.

In the area of administrative department assessment, this concern might take shape as follows:

> The student personnel team has had several meetings in which the issue of student displeasure about student housing has been voiced. Several questions emerge in team discussion including, "Is our housing substandard? If so, what needs to be done? If not, what is it that is generating this loud set of complaints?"

Such questions lead to step number two.

In the second assessment step of **data collection**, responsible parties determine appropriate procedures to gather good data and then gather it.

On the basis of several conversations in committee meetings, the student personnel team decides to put into place a broad-based <u>student survey</u> to determine student opinion. They also decide to run a series of <u>focus interviews</u> with student clusters currently living in housing. They also commission a <u>housing audit</u> done pro bono by one of the governing board members who has expertise in this area.

Once such data are collected and organized into a semi-processed format, the third assessment step involves **interpretive conversations** and the generation of possible solutions/ideas.

The student personnel team spends one committee meeting working through the data and organizing them into recurring themes. They discover roughly six major issues; one has to do with the building; the other five have to do with those persons who work with the building or with the students who live there. The team fashions three feasible "big" options that could deal at some expense with the physical building. They also name sixteen "small" options/tactics that might be used to address the personnel issues. These options range from policy changes and job description adjustments to closer supervision and changed responsibilities for the dean of students. The committee writes up a report summarizing these conclusions/proposals.

The fourth assessment step, **strategic choice/tactical implementation,** has do with governance, decision-making, and putting into place adequate persons and procedures to make something happen. Strategic choices have to do with deciding what "we" will do. This is where proposals are put into dialogue with broader missional and constituency concerns. Given the meta-context of such conversation, strategic choices are made, specific tactics are then put into place, and accountability is secured by designating persons who are to have oversight and responsibility for the process.

The student personnel team's report comes, via the dean of students, into the president's council. The council agrees with the team's diagnosis and proposals, forwarding its approval to the school's governing board, which then adds one proposal about the building to the silent capital fund campaign while also deciding that the team's "smaller" options/ideas about personnel should be immediately implemented. The president, chief financial officer, and building manager are told to "make it so," and to report back on progress made to the governing board in six months.

As noted above, the fourth step does not end "assessment" per se but results in certain improvements that must themselves be assessed. The process is open-ended and on-going.

Understanding, and not misunderstanding, the assessment "loop"

It is, then, best to conceive of assessment, not as a linear process with a discrete beginning and end, but as a "loop." Given areas of the school in which standards associated with good practice are known, these four steps form an assessment "loop" that looks like this:

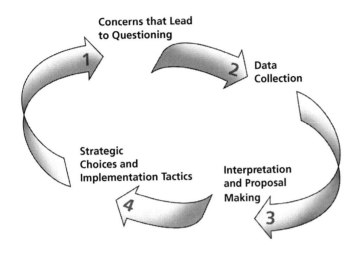

I intend this rendering of the "loop" as a heuristic device, an artificial teaching example that, while too simplistic to describe any actual situation, breaks down the process of assessment into four understandable component parts. As such, it can be helpful for those who are trying, for the first time, to understand the process of assessment. It can also, however, become harmful to that process when used prescriptively.

Those who have engaged in assessment work for some time will note that, in practice, the "loop" ends up looking more like a spiral, as numerous "loops" are always being traced and any particular loop begins again as soon as it ends. So, too, those engaged in assessment can enter the loop at almost any point. I would also suggest that when fully embraced, the woodenness of the four-step approach disappears, and the assessment process becomes an organic part of the "assessment culture" of the school; that is, "this is how we do it."

Accrediting concern #1: evidence

When visiting a school, the accrediting committee will want to see evidence that such a system of loops exists. This means, among other things, that in each area there is a reasonable structure (understood, named, and in place) that notes the "who, what, where, when, and how" in relation to each of the four steps. In this regard, accreditors mistrust the usefulness of a structure that is not clearly defined or that assumes one person will "do" assessment. Accreditors also assume (in much the same fashion that a homeowner assumes a house should not leak like a sieve) that standards associated with the good practices of higher education should be clearly articulated in every institution.

While accreditors hold a "culture of assessment" as the ideal, this ideal assumes multiple levels of engagement, numerous persons so engaged, and a clear record of assessment strategies, tactics, and choices that are understood to be the result of a cyclical, routine plan of assessment embraced by the school.

Accrediting concern #2: "closing the loop"

The visiting accrediting committee will also want to see how the school uses this "loop." It is incumbent on accreditors to ask if the assessment loop that has been described to them is not only in place (i.e., show us the plan), but, indeed, whether the loop has been "closed" (i.e., has the plan been fully implemented?). By this they mean that they want to see evidence that all four assessment steps have taken place in any given assessment process. All too often accreditors experience schools that ask questions and generate data that are ignored, stored in files, or remain in unread initial "reports." When these things occur, the assessment "loop" has not been "closed."

Leaving the loop "open" is often the result of not defining a specific location (such as the president's cabinet or council) that regularly monitors the strategic, decision-making processes throughout the institution and maintains on their agenda a regular review of the accountability structures and personnel who are to proceed with implementation.

"Closing the loop" moves the gathered data (from steps one and two) through a number of interpretive proposals (step three) into the strategic decision-making and tactical implementation stage (step four); not closing the loop looks like this:

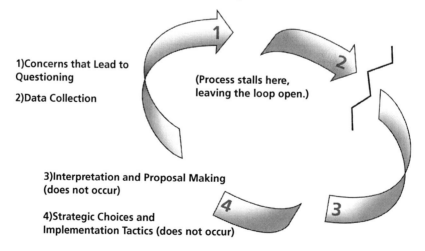

1)Concerns that Lead to Questioning

2)Data Collection

(Process stalls here, leaving the loop open.)

3)Interpretation and Proposal Making (does not occur)

4)Strategic Choices and Implementation Tactics (does not occur)

Stalling at points two and three

Accreditors often encounter schools that seem to be good at collecting data, but poor at moving that data from step two into step three, the place where appropriate venues interpret data and generate initial proposals. Accreditors who see stacks of computer print-outs gathering dust in cardboard boxes know that something got stalled, and that the loop has not been closed.

Alternatively, data gets collected and initial proposals are generated by appropriate venues, but then the proposals languish on someone's desk. Again, the loop remains open, and the opportunity to engage new strategies that would foster the school's fulfillment of its mission remain untried.

Toward closing the loop

A school working at closing the loop in departmental assessment, for example, is able to point to a regular meeting where the "loop" is applied to concerns and issues that arise in each department. And, if an accreditor were to ask how that "worked," someone interviewed from the school about the assessment "loop" could offer something like the following as an account of the school's departmental assessment process:

We're aware of what good practice with assessment means (or should mean) for schools like us. There are certain standards that we can use to gauge where we are. Anyway, we'd like to assume that we can always do better. Step one, **questioning** occurs most often during departmental meetings. The questions we asked this past year were specifically related to the accreditation process. We read the accreditation expectations, and our concerns often evolved into one or two tightly constructed questions. Then we would ask, "Can the department get help in constructing a tool to help us get this data?" In this school we know several persons who stand willing to help. As the questions become more clear, step two **(data collection)** unfolds. One or more specific procedures for data collection are put into place; people carefully define the process. Raw data are collected and initially organized into a semi-processed fashion, and then moved into step three, **interpretation and proposal making**. Our originating departmental committee then wades through the data. We ask, "What do those data mean? What do these data tell us? What might these data lead us to propose? Would our proposal(s) answer our original concern? Are there deeper concerns here? Are we ready to offer suggestions as to what would be helpful here? Do we know about other, better models that address our concerns?" This meaning-making activity may take more time and involve more questioning and more data collection, but eventually one or more ideas take shape and emerge as useful proposals. These proposals make their way to the location where decisions in our school often occur—the president's council. Step four, **determining strategic**

choices and deciding implementation tactics, is logically what the president's council does in our school. If departmental assessment is to continue to be an important and intentional process in our school, the president's council will continue to regularly schedule agenda time to make step four decisions in light of our mission plan, our constituencies, and our current agenda in the seminary.

Because the president's cabinet is the place where key administrators gather who are charged with running the school, numerous issues often arise there when the assessment process is made more intentional. The student personnel department's concern regarding housing (noted earlier in this chapter) is one such example.

The president's council

Most accrediting committees assume that the core of the school's assessment pattern is driven by the president because assessment is understood as requiring due diligence from the president (and the board). Accreditors, further, assume that an examination of evidence from the president's cabinet or council will be the primary step in determining whether or not intentional assessment occurs at the school. The cabinet not only sets the tone, they believe, but also promotes the usefulness of such a systemic approach. If there is no evidence of regularized assessment in the agendas or minutes of cabinet meetings (particularly related to the accreditation process), most accreditors will find talk of an assessment plan suspect.

Further, accreditors will assume that major assessment proposals needing board approval often will first appear in the minutes of the president's council and can be traced as they move to the board level.

Accreditors also will be interested in how the president keeps such proposals connected to the big picture; that is, does the president position each major proposal within missional priorities and the contextual realities facing the school?

Out of this confluence it is presumed that the president's cabinet will reach strategic choices. Some plans or proposals will be rejected, others will be approved. Implementation plans will be discussed. Accountability issues will be decided. If the proposal involves governance issues, the council may determine that the overall plan will now move into the committee structure of the governing board, and the school moves forward.

While the example used above regarding student housing is drawn from the area of departmental assessment, there are other major areas (for example, student learning assessment and academic degree program assessment) in which assessment might take other forms, but the "loop" of assessment remains in play and is not abandoned.

What we have learned

Simply put, accrediting agencies expect every school to have incorporated the assessment process into every aspect of institutional life. Good (and appropriate) assessment assumes a positive institutional ethos. The president has a key role in affirming and making certain the school uses reasonable and appropriate assessment procedures. Faculty and administrative resentment about assessment can occur because assessment is felt to be an intrusion that is overly prescriptive and entirely numerically based. These arguments are red herrings. Assessment occurs whenever humans gather.

The assessment process in a school is a refined version of what we do as a matter of course in everyday living. In either our homes or institutions, assessment can be thoughtless or quite intentional. One buys a shoe too hastily, and it causes blisters. Unfortunately, the penalty for poor assessment at the institutional level is much greater than blistered feet! Thoughtful assessment patterns can usefully engage multiple levels of the institution in decision-making, and, accordingly, offer (at a particular moment) a genuine method for determining strategic priorities. In the end, an assessment process such as we are discussing allows the school to fulfill its mission, while remaining healthy and strong.

CHAPTER 2

STUDENT LEARNING ASSESSMENT: THE MDIV DEGREE

I think I bit off more than I can chew.
I tried to take three courses this quarter,
and the many papers, teaching parish duties,
and the kids' illnesses have nearly driven me crazy.

A single mother who is also a seminary student[2]

When a theological school receives a visit from an accreditation evaluation committee, that committee will assume that the school not only has adopted an assessment plan, but can provide evidence that will demonstrate implementation of the plan for more than one cycle. All such accreditation visits are very concerned that such a plan is in place and working when it comes to student learning assessment.

Student learning assessment is about the learning of individual students. When students enter a degree program, that degree program should state which learning objectives make up the degree program and when and how each student in the degree program will be engaged in a learning assessment process in accordance with those objectives. The accreditor will ask to see (1) the degree objectives, (2) how those objectives are carried out in the degree structures (courses, practicums, etc.), and (3) when and how each and every student's learning in the degree regularly is assessed with the student actively participating in that assessment.

Constructive versus summative approaches

There is an argument regarding student learning assessment between those who follow a constructive approach and those who follow a summative approach. **Constructivists** tend to regard assessment as a tool to help adults build, at least in part, the trajectory of their own learning experience. **Summative** adherents tend to consider assessment as that which happens *to* students instead of *with* students. They look back in judgment at what has/has not been accomplished. They strongly rely on data that are reached by reliance upon whether or not a student satisfies a school's pre-set learning objectives. It is clear to them that learning outcomes define the terrain that all students must navigate.

There are true believers on both sides. It would be unfortunate were theological educators to succumb to a too easily drawn polarity such as this one. Nevertheless, schools must negotiate the issues that accompany this argument.

A "middle way"

Theological educators readily admit, however, that having learning outcomes can provide both students and professors with a helpful map of a degree program's educational expectations. They also admit that summative judgments linked and informed by such objectives do not necessarily block or impede a constructive understanding as to how individual students can better connect with and come to build appropriate learning possibilities.

A "middle way" also understands that there is a theological imperative for elders in a learning community to tell the truth with those students under their supervision in the learning process. Connecting summative concerns within an individual's discernment process cannot mean that whatever is being constructively decided by the student necessarily trumps the findings of communal discernment, in other words, a summative judgment.

In this regard, sometimes a summative conversation can connect in vocationally helpful ways with adult-informed communal truth-telling. Not every person enrolled in a course-of-study belongs there, and it sometimes takes an act of faith to name out loud (in a middler exam, for example) that which is already understood with great clarity by a student.

Some schools do this review within the framework of specific courses, as a part of field education, or as part of a formative practicum of some sort; others do it only at the end of the first and second year, with a senior capstone course and/or exit interview/exam. Still others do a strong, initial screening coupled with a very serious intake process and seminar. These schools often add a "middler review" and a senior exit exam/interview to this process. Some do it only as an ongoing assessment process. What is crucial is that whatever process is used be openly named within the catalog or student handbook that describes this degree and that the same process be applied to every student in the degree. This usually translates to a "student assessment tracking sheet" in the name of each student that is kept in the registrar's office on computer or in secure hard copy, plus a confidential file (portfolio) containing all papers associated with this process for each student.

Student assessment and the MDiv degree

Every school engages in a variety of procedures from which evidence of student learning can be derived. Often the school does not make good use of procedures already in place that could be applied to this task. For example, many schools have admission records that include academic, spiritual, and personal autobiographical information. Letters of endorsement and recommendation are often included from pastors or home church officers. Some schools note on their admission form that if a student is accepted, the student's submitted data will be used in the student's assessment program in the school. Some schools bring these data into advisory one-on-one and group conversations during intake courses that frame the seminary experience for the new student while also introducing new areas of learning (like spiritual formation and how a seminary helps a student to acquire tools for contextual ministry). Some schools use a variety of vocational, psychological, and academic exams as part of this intake experience. All such work could be argued as *establishing a baseline* with entering MDiv students, but it only becomes part of the assessment process if and when these data are critically reflected upon by the student, persons like the student's advisor, and those who have been charged with the responsibility for interpreting such tests.

Establishing a baseline

Establishing a baseline for each student means working through a process in which both student and school come to know what the student brings to the particular learning outcomes associated with this academic program.[3] A part of developing this process depends on the school's clarity in establishing course objectives (more on this in Chapter Three). Such defining occurs as student and school representatives sort through data that result from the merger of the various instruments or procedures noted above. There are informal and formal ways this occurs.

Informal ways include anecdotal observation and conversational moments noted by advisors, yet still recognized as part of the evaluative process. For example, one student engages her history professor in pre-class conversations every week; the professor quickly discovers that the student has a PhD in history and has served as a lay leader in a key congregation known well by the professor. In addition, this student gives evidence in class of knowledge accompanied by social awareness. Without arrogance, the student demonstrates competent leadership in the academic setting. Accordingly, the history professor discusses this student (again, informally) with other faculty members.

Such informal observations on the part of the one professor are brought to bear in more **formal** occasions when conversation with a student occurs during a structured moment around a set of specific goals; for example, sorting through the data in the individual's official file with her/his advisor, and perhaps others, to clarify the student's learning location in conjunction with the learning goals/objectives/understandings that the student's course of study is built to accomplish.

At the onset of such review, a student is often invited to prepare a brief paper summarizing his or her learning base or trajectory and how he or she thinks it might (best) play out during the proposed course of study. The paper may be distributed in advance of the initial school/student formal meeting. As that meeting unfolds, notes are taken and later edited into a document signed by both the student and the school representatives. This document summarizes the group's collective interpretation of the data they have discussed with the student. Specific proposals are included; for example, in relation to the student who entered with an earned PhD in history, conversation was held about the student's future vocation. Because of the student's previous work in history and because the student wants to become a parish pastor, several required courses were waived with substitute courses suggested that were deemed more appropriate for the student's learning trajectory. Another student, wanting to be a pastor but having had no church experience, is asked to join a local church and to anticipate enrollment in a particular field education practicum by keeping a personal journal about the experience of being new in a local church.

In both cases, the student emerges from this formal conversation with a document that the student will be expected to sign summarizing the student's learning objectives. The aim of such formal conversations is to not only establish a collective understanding of what the student brings to this course of study, but also to push/lure/suggest further avenues of learning that can be done within the learning objectives understood by the school as appropriate to this particular student in this particular degree.

As noted above, no two schools approach "baseline conversations" in the same way. Some schools assume assessment happens "naturally" and point to informal, anecdotal "evidence" (such as was described above). Other schools build elaborate testing programs, but often fail to interpret to each student the results of such procedures within the learning objectives of the program. Some schools wait until a half-way point (middler review) to hold their first formal conversation with a student. Still others fold all formal conversations into an entry "seminar/practicum" that includes conversation about "learning objectives" and helping students write individual "learning covenants."

Accreditors will ask how a school intentionally assesses student learning. Key evidence that they would be looking for includes a series of well-defined and regular, summative occasions, when every new student is mandated to attend an individualized, formal meeting with the express goal of understanding where they are located within the learning aims and goals of the particular course of study. These might be scheduled, for example, at the end of the intake course, and at the end of the first quarter or first year. [Note that while this book explicitly refers to the MDiv course of study, all seminary courses of study leading to approved degrees are expected to have learning goals and stated procedures for assessing student learning.]

Academic deans in large schools sometimes groan as they count the cost of providing such assessment procedures. Again, the issue of *mission* emerges; if the school is intent on providing ministerial education via an MDiv program, resources adequate to this task should be deployed by the school. Frankly, this issue often gets framed by faculty as an unwarranted incursion into their time. Academic deans of small, medium, and large schools very quickly become aware of faculty "load" issues when discussing student learning assessment procedures, but those schools where such processes are in place are equally quick to note that "after all, *student learning* is our business."

Those in the interview or review with the student

Schools with experience in such baseline conversations indicate that no fewer than two school representatives should be engaged in the interview with a student. For some schools this is a set team; for other schools the persons who meet with the student are uniquely tailored to the perceived learning issues of the student. For example, one student might have a conversation with an academic advisor, a field education director, and the person responsible for interpreting the initial vocational test battery. Another student might get these three plus the academic dean. The crucial thing is that those present are chosen in ways that are consistent with the school's published protocols regarding such meetings.

Schools accordingly involve different persons in these meetings, depending on the learning objectives of the course of study and those intimately engaged with both the program and with a specific student in the program. Several persons who might be included come to mind—the student's academic advisor, the faculty responsible for the MDiv intake seminar/retreat, the person responsible for interpreting entering test scores, the field education/clinical placement director, the director of the MDiv course of study, the dean of students/chapel, and the person charged with spiritual/character formation.

Some schools have configured their MDiv course of study so that a mentoring experience is used at the beginning of the MDiv program to bring students into contact with area pastors. These schools engage students and pastors in an educational process that brings them together in numerous ways early on in the student's seminary career. Some schools do such mentoring primarily during the intake seminar that runs for a full quarter or semester. Other schools follow this practice but add to it a common retreat. Still others utilize their mentoring pastors in conjunction with a broader based field education program throughout each student's seminary career. These schools attest that these pastors are invaluable resources in accomplishing educational outcomes or objectives with students. They also note that the cost of involving pastors in this fashion seems to be offset by increased giving by the particular congregations from which the pastors have been engaged.

Portfolios/files/learning covenants

Whatever the configuration of those in the interview with the student, a candid assessment of what the student brings to the learning objectives of the course of study (and where/how the student might be pushed by the school's learning objectives at the edges of the student's knowledge/skills/being) is helped by good data and a clear set of expectations as to the goal of such meetings. Some schools have decided that two such meetings in the "life" of the student are sufficient. As mentioned above, other schools differ, each according to the philosophy underlying their process of assessment, but all schools keep records derived from such meetings. Some schools call the records *portfolios*, others refer to them as the student's *file* or *learning covenant.*

For some schools, the files are maintained electronically. For other schools, the file is a hard copy, manila file. By whatever method, the school needs to determine, perhaps with input from the student, what kind of material should appear in the file.

Some schools include only data compiled via the school's official processes. This might mean, for example, that over the life of the student's program, documents such as CPE reports, denominational ordination letters of recommendation, academic transcripts, parish field education evaluations, seminar/immersion pass/fail reflections by faculty, internship/special project reports, and position-in-ministry senior examination papers are added to the file.

Some schools also include all official correspondence from the school to the student (letters indicating fellowships, scholarships, discipline results, awarded honors, etc.). Other schools assume that graduate-level students ought to be engaged in a regular, ongoing constructive selection of additional data. Accordingly, these schools encourage students to include things like their learning covenants from years one, two, and three within their file. Exemplary papers, videos of exemplary sermons, faculty commended papers, and examples of *critical instance in ministry* reports or tapes are also included. What a student offers in terms of the student's integration in the learning process, in light of the learning objectives of the degree, often are bolstered by such materials chosen as evidence and included in the file by the student.

How much (or how little) choice the student is allowed in relation to what sort of data is placed in the file is usually determined by the school's understanding of the role students have in their own learning.

A gateway to "candidacy"

Some schools see the "middler review" of the student as the place where the student's understanding of learning progress is made and the school's understanding of learning are aligned with a judgment to be made. Until the middler review, these schools call each student a "student." Learning covenants, accordingly, are flexible documents, but with the middler review comes the judgment that most (but not all) "students" are moved into "candidacy" status. Before this formal meeting they were students, but now they are "candidates for the degree." Whatever papers emerge from this meeting, therefore, include plans for completing the course of study. With learning objectives in mind, such plans might mandate completion of additional courses, practica, immersions, field education, counseling, or spiritual direction. Such plans are the direct result of student learning assessment, but with candidacy determined, now have a more formal aspect to them. Graduation seems closer!

For some students, however, candidacy is not attained. For whatever reasons, these students are advised to move toward other vocations or to engage in certain programs or experiences outside the seminary and then return to pursue candidacy status. Again, such decisions (when students are deemed partners in this process) are often more easily reached by the student on the basis of specific learning objectives not attained. Often, such conversations are mutual and everyone (including the student) recognizes that this course of study is not a "good fit." Occasionally, however, the conversation is difficult. Usually the academic dean is an engaged participant in such conversations. Again, published protocols naming (for every student) expectations around the middler review are critical to both the student and the school in defining this as a reasonable and helpful process.

Assessing student learning before graduation

As students move toward graduation, schools frame the student learning assessment process in a variety of ways. Informal assessment continues, as do a number of more formal patterns of assessment. In schools where a portfolio/file system engages students and appropriate school representatives in an ongoing system of assessment, collected data continue to be interpreted through one or more meeting points. Such meetings frequently occur at the three-quarter mark of the senior year, however that date is calibrated (and part-time students might discover that they meet in times other than January). Other schools see the exit interview/exam on the candidate's position paper as their concluding occasion for the assessment of an individual student's learning.

Still others have what assessment experts label a "capstone" course in which individual student's integrative position papers make use of learnings acquired during their course of study. "Hearings" in this course sometimes are a part of peer examination of each person's position paper, and an oral hearing with a panel of professors serves as a closing "interview" regarding his/her learning experience at this school. Some see the "exit interview" as a separable moment, which is the responsibility of the president, while the oral position paper exam is the capstone moment where faculty assess each student's learning as framed by the learning objectives of the program. Again, the nature of an exam is that some may fall short—not graduate, but be asked to pursue more education toward one or more learning objectives (various responses can be seen in this regard, but many schools report that their "hard-edged" decision occurs not at this moment, but at the middler review). Both the capstone exam and/or the middler review are examples of summative assessment—a consideration of what has occurred, rather than what *might* have occurred.

The four steps of the student learning assessment loop

Intentional assessment of student learning can be said to move increasingly from the informal, anecdotal style into a more formal time and place in which the "loop" of assessment can easily be described: (1) **questioning**: "What are some ways learning is occurring for you in regard to both your learning objectives and the learning outcomes or objectives of this course of study?; (2) **gathering data**: "Can we bring together widely scattered data into files or portfolios that provide evidence of your learning as you fulfill the expected outcomes?"; (3) **interpreting/proposing**: "When wrestled with, do such data yield understanding as to your strengths, weaknesses, and growing edges as well as allow us to make good proposals toward clarifying your personal learning trajectory?"; (4) **strategic choices/implementations**: "And, does your trajectory of learning have specific occasions when serious consideration is focused on you in light of program learning outcomes, and can deliberate decisions be reached that help you in your educational journey?"

When an accreditation committee arrives on campus, it will assign someone the task of determining how (or if) student learning assessment occurs on this campus. Often, an academic dean on the visiting committee draws this assignment. That academic dean initially will spend time pursuing this concern with the school's academic dean, but will move beyond the dean into the various administrative and faculty offices until clarity emerges as to the school's process of student learning assessment. Once this picture has been clarified, the dean will move into conversations about the topic with students across the various degrees offered at the school. A visiting assessment committee member dialogue with a student can be imagined:

Committee member:	"Tell me how your learning is being assessed in the MDiv program here."
Student:	"As I understand it (and I am in my second year here), there

	are three major moments of assessment—one at the end of my first year (which I have done); one at the three-quarter mark of year two (which I am getting ready to do); and finally at the three-quarter mark of year three, my senior year."
Committee member:	"What happened in the 'moment' at the end of your first year?"
Student:	"We had been instructed in our first course on the importance of a portfolio being used in tracking our learning in the MDiv program. We spent a lot of time in that course discussing learning outcomes associated with MDiv program objectives and how we personally were positioned regarding each one. Both my advisor and I met fairly often that first year, and she encouraged me to focus on using the portfolio to demonstrate my own progress in relation to three of those objectives. In fact, we decided that those three objectives were very useful in determining what progress I was making in my own education here."
Committee member:	"So I'm hearing that you had an entry course in which you discussed the school's objectives for the MDiv course of study, and that you and your advisor determined that concentrating on three of those learning objectives would help you decide what?"
Student:	"She and I talked a lot about my educational journey here. Most of my first year courses were pretty well set by the school, but the papers I did in two of the courses were negotiated by my desire to push my learning and to pull me in line with the three MDiv course of study objectives. I came to school as a recent convert, so the deep history of the Christian tradition is unknown to me. I told my history professor that I needed to read more and do more in his class. I think he and I figured out a good way to frame my reading; I wrote a good paper; it's in my portfolio. I also asked the history professor to include a note in the portfolio about my progress."
Committee member:	"What did the meeting that year look like?"
Student:	"There were four people there: me, my advisor, one of the team that taught my first course, and the one pastor I was assigned to 'shadow' as a part of that course.

We met for an hour and a half. I think they had a format they used, but, whether or not they did, I do know that we spent most of our time talking about me—what I knew I came into the MDiv program and what I've learned since I've been here. We talked a lot about how I did regarding specific outcomes connected to my courses, and they noted several upcoming courses that could help me complete the objectives of this degree. They told me my advisor would write up the conversation and then share that document with me. That did occur, and then I was asked to respond in writing. I also did that."

Committee member: "Apart from looking at what had already happened, was there any future planning or suggestions made to you?"

Student: "Yeah. Curiously enough, the best idea for my learning edge came from the pastor I had shadowed. He suggested that when I took the second year course on congregational life that my major paper might focus on my work with him in his church. I got very excited by that prospect, and I can tell you today that I am engaged in the course, and he and I are having a very good time looking at some of the course theories in light of our shared congregational experience! Again, as a recent convert, church life is very strange to me!"

What we have learned

Student assessment focuses on student learning. Schools are to have appropriate student learning assessment plans in place for each degree program they offer. Establishing a baseline for a specific student's learning allows the student, along with appropriate school personnel, to determine those learning experiences (e.g., practica, seminars, courses, field education) that best educate the student in conjunction with the learning goals/objectives/understandings that the student's course of study is built to accomplish.

Some schools do only *constructive* student assessment, while others do only *summative* assessment. Schools emphasizing ongoing constructive assessment tend to engage both student and school in the process; schools emphasizing only summative assessment tend to see assessment as something solely done by the school. Other schools mix these formats, encouraging students and school representatives to work together at ongoing student learning assessment punctuated by occasional summative moments like a middler review or senior exams.

In all instances, however, the four steps of the assessment "loop" apply: (1) posing good questions; (2) collecting good data; (3) interpreting the data; and (4) making good choices and implementing them. "Closing the loop" occurs when the student and seminary personnel get together around evidence of the student's learning trajectory. While no two schools structure these meetings in exactly the same way, most require that decisions reached in those venues be documented. Some form of student file becomes a repository for decisions reached; accordingly, confidentiality must be assured.

In this regard, the accreditation visitor could use the above conversation with a student as part of the basis on which to judge the effectiveness of the school's implementation of its learning assessment procedures. The conversation appears to demonstrate that the school is intentional about having learning outcomes in place and regularly used in assessing student learning. The school appears to be carefully implementing a defined process that helps students understand the implications of what has been learned.

The student learning assessment process should always follow a regularized format. When the format of the process is printed (e.g., in a student handbook and/or school catalog), protocols are understood and everyone has a common set of expectations. When schools do not have a common template for student learning assessment, decisions as to what matters in a student's personal course of study increasingly rely on informal, idiosyncratic data. Members of a visiting accreditation committee are likely to ask the faculty to develop a clearer, intentional explanation regarding student learning assessment.

CHAPTER 3

ASSESSING THE ACADEMIC PROGRAM: THE ACADEMIC DEAN

The language we use to describe disciplinary interactions
does not help, for it moves in a distinctly military register,
drawing on the lexicon of conflict and contestation. We have
"turf wars" and inhabit "territories," "bastions," and "fiefdoms."
We "jealously guard" and "police" our discipline against
"incursions" and worry about "border traffic," "intellectual migration,"
and "boundary crossing."

Maria Tatar[4]

The president of a theological school often relies upon the academic dean to drive both the student learning and academic program assessment processes. While the president has primary responsibility for the overall institutional assessment process of the school, the academic dean is often expected to have both the knowledge and expertise to educate the school in these processes and to ready the school for the accreditation evaluation visits every ten years.

While a school's assessment program is intended to keep all institutional constituents informed about how students are/are not engaged in the learning process, about what broader contextual indicators mean for the school's educational mission, and about ways in which the academic program might be made better, the academic dean usually comes to the job with little or no background in assessment. This is through no real fault of the dean.

Deans sometimes emerge from within a faculty, often because the faculty recognizes in one or more of its members nascent capabilities for administration, educational imagination, and trustworthiness. If a dean emerges in this fashion, the faculty may see the new dean as "their" dean in any contestation with the administration or the board. This, despite the fact that most deans in theological education serve at the will of the president and by a vote of confirmation by the board. Nevertheless, the new dean becomes structurally positioned between faculty and the president. While the president is perceived as having authority via the board, the dean's authority is primarily seen as being derived from the faculty.

Because of these issues, some schools have turned to outside hires or to more clear-cut appointment processes linking the dean to the board and president. While governance boundaries appear, in these instances, to have been more clearly drawn, faculty members may resist such moves by digging in their heels and passively resisting all changes suggested by this "interloper."

A culture of assessment: becoming a learning community

Because of such complexities, the academic dean who works in a trusting relationship with president, board, and faculty often faces a difficult relational task in matters of assessment (and accreditation).

Assessment, the dean may well suggest, is much more than accreditation. Unless the school is in the accreditation doghouse, the accreditation visitors will only visit the school once every ten years. In contrast, assessment, the dean will argue, is an everyday process that when appropriately done will result in a school that knows itself better and can provide to the church graduates that effectively embody the school's mission. However, such a strong claim by the dean can only be supported by both the dean and the faculty if the claim "works."

In this regard, the dean will argue that an effective culture of learning, occasioned in part by embracing a good assessment process, cannot be built if a school engages in intentional assessment only in order to jump through the accreditation hoop once every ten years. A positive "learning/assessment culture" occurs step by small step over time, and its value accordingly must be regularly demonstrated. The dean's task in all this, made delicate and complex by faculty fear, deep resistance, and ignorance, is to work steadily toward the regular implementation of a simple assessment plan.

Moving towards a shared culture of intentional assessment requires intentionality and diplomacy. A wise first step is for the dean to help the faculty articulate what the school already is doing in assessing student learning. By naming such steps that already exist, the dean discovers how one or two additional steps might effectively *strengthen* what is already in place. And then the dean encourages those most closely connected with the plan over the next few years to assess the plan's effectiveness. Through such a simple process, a "team" begins (with the dean) to "own" the emergent plan. And no plan is a perfect plan; what the dean (and the team) aspire to is a *good enough plan* that appropriately inculcates the values of the school's educational mission as currently understood.

Three assessment areas for which the dean is responsible

The dean should understand that there are three separate concerns that must be addressed in any effective assessment plan. First, the school needs to be clear as to how it approaches *student learning assessment* (see Chapter Two). Second, the school should become more intentional about *academic program assessment* (the primary concern of this chapter). Third, the dean has a number of tasks that have to do with overall *institutional assessment* (examples of this will be discussed at the end of this chapter). These three areas, while discrete, often overlap.

While some of the principles employed in student learning assessment also are appropriate to academic program assessment, each area has particular concerns at issue as well. Student learning assessment focuses on students while academic program assessment focuses on the specific set of academic programs that are offered by the school. In similar fashion, institutional assessment involves looking at every single institutional area, but its focus is much broader than the concerns of any one division or department of the school.

Because student learning assessment was described in detail in Chapter Two, the focus of this chapter is *academic program and the dean's role in institutional assessment*. Both of these areas will be presented from the academic dean's perspective.

Constructing an academic program assessment plan

The academic dean is responsible for academic program assessment. Accreditors will be quick to point out that each program leading to a degree must have a functional assessment plan in hand, and must be able to provide evidence that the plan is being continuously implemented.

Such plans often begin with the school's mission statement. Working with the faculty, the dean connects missional concepts and learning outcomes to the educational goals of each degree program. For example, one broadly descriptive *learning goal* for an MDiv course of study might be "the student will have an increased capacity for ministerial and public leadership." That goal would then be translated into outcomes that not only can be readily observed and documented, but also can be reflected upon and named in formal assessment procedures with the student and the student's faculty advisor. In this process, the dean makes certain that the mission of the school informs each learning outcome so that a student can be directly assessed in this regard via course-work, practica, or other educational experiences.

There are various terms used by theological schools to describe their MDiv degree's *learning goals* (outcomes, objectives, learnings). These goals are the responsibility of the faculty to determine. The overall process of connecting an institution's mission statement to the expectations underlying each degree program accordingly takes time to accomplish.

Schools who have worked through the steps of this task usually indicate that defining the learning goals for the MDiv degree took two years. This appears to be a minimum time frame for accomplishing this task.

As one school began to work through the steps, they employed three faculty members whose discipline was education. The dean asked them to front-load the process with their production of single-page *"springboard" discussion papers* detailing some of the arguments that they anticipated would occur during this process. The dean accordingly shuffled committee projects and cut back on faculty loads so that *regular meetings* to discuss those topics could emerge over the two-year span with the full attendance of the faculty. Recognizing that some cumulative time needed to be focused on the strands of thought that such discussions produced, the dean additionally set aside a mix of one and two-day retreats during which a kind of consensus emerged over critical issues that had been raised during the year.

While such a process appears, at least on paper, to be benign, the dean expended a lot of social capital in seeing it through. This happened because not everyone is ever on the same page, and because some of the professors did not want to affirm the faculty position on learning that seemed to be emerging.

Curriculum revision

Making clear connections between the school's mission and the learning objectives of each degree program produces its own set of curricular questions. No dean wants to instigate a turf war among faculty and their guilds, but curricular revisioning almost always leads to such a moment unless a rapprochement can be reached via a faculty's shared vision and understanding of a common mission. If, for example, "ministry" is understood as what a school teaches, then those faculty who accepted positions at a particular school can move forward in their teaching within a common understanding of their corporate mission. But even then, as schools attempt to connect learning goals to specific degree programs (as they must), deans (and faculty) always discover that this process leads to curriculum revision, whether or not they agree about the educational task or the vocation of a theological educator.

A happy ending is not always the result of such a process, no matter how much time or intentional thought precedes it.

Faced with such concerns, the thoughtful dean employs a model like the one described above:
• get some key faculty on board early on, asking them to help shape the process by drafting relevant discussion papers for the whole faculty;

- cut back on some of the faculty committee loads that always stress faculty members;
- in advance design regular conversational occasions so that salient issues can emerge;
- provide occasional one or two-day retreats where substantial time can be directed at emerging issues;
- understand (and give voice to) the individual and collective concerns that will emerge;
- recognizing that complete consensus is unlikely, move forward into a common understanding, so that, at the end, it should be possible for the full faculty to say together: "This is who we are. This is what we do. This is how we educate/prepare our students"; and, finally,
- realize that the resultant two years is both an investment in assessment and the beginning of a curricular revisioning process that will (it is hoped) result in a new curriculum (which itself will need to be assessed).

Given all this, it is important to note that the school discussed above instituted such a proactive process carefully only after framing it as an intellectual task (and not as a mandatory accreditation requirement or as some new idea by the dean about "outcomes assessment").

Learning goals/outcomes

Accreditors suggest that learning goals or outcomes should be readily understood and clearly stated. Some schools post expected learning outcomes for each degree's program on their website. For example, here are the MDiv learning objectives at New Orleans Baptist Theological Seminary:

All graduates are expected to have at least a minimum level of competency in all of the following seven areas:
Biblical Exposition
     To interpret and communicate the Bible accurately.
Christian Theological Heritage
     To understand and interpret Christian theological heritage and Baptist polity for the church.
Disciple Making
     To stimulate church health through mobilizing the church for missions, evangelism, discipleship, and church growth.
Interpersonal Skills
     To perform pastoral care effectively, with skills in communication and conflict management.
Servant Leadership
     To serve churches effectively through team ministry.
Spiritual and Character Formation

To provide moral leadership by modeling and mentoring Christian character and devotion.

Worship Leadership

To facilitate worship effectively.

Given specific degree programs, no two schools will envision identical learning goals for the MDiv program, and this is a good thing. Most schools see the defining of learning goals for the MDiv as faculty work, and accordingly keep this process pretty much in-house. Other schools open the process to various constituencies. Some open the process only near its end, using alumnae or judicatory committees as sounding boards that offer comments to fine tune the faculty's work. Others invite comment in the middle of the process from focus groups composed of graduates, current students, and persons who employ graduates of the school. A few schools design survey instruments that give graduates and other constituencies or stakeholders appropriate platforms to express what they believe the degree should focus on as goals or objectives. Still others ask specific graduates (i.e., a "purposive sample") to write commentaries that might serve as initial discussion papers for those faculty working on the faculty agenda in this area. All such indirect measures are useful in that they provide information regarding what various stakeholders or constituencies value, or have found lacking, in the structure of a particular degree program.

For example, a pastor with ten years of thoughtful ministry was asked to reflect on what had made her a good minister. Her response was that she had learned the following skills through her seminary MDiv program and her ten years of pastoral experience: 1) taking initiative without taking over; 2) thinking theologically about situations and decisions; 3) facilitating small groups—task and process oriented; 4) responding to people in crisis with appropriate care; 5) ritualizing such needs through both personal and corporate worship; 6) mobilizing people to action in response to needs of individuals, local communities, and the wider world; 7) negotiating the politics of church and denomination; 8) making connections between people, resources, and visions that are both empowering and sustaining; and 9) caring for her own vocational well-being by attending to her spiritual, psychological, and physical health.[5]

In the language of this chapter, she presented nine learning goals (or competencies, objectives, or outcomes) that she values and believes ought to occur within the MDiv course-of-study. By so doing, she highlights the necessity of thinking theologically, understanding the context of ministry, being equipped with the tools of ministry, and being able to appropriately exercise leadership skills in an integrative fashion within the context(s) of ministry.

While her insights into learning goals or objectives for the MDiv degree could be added to or subtracted from, most of them would be affirmed by faculty from many schools as laudable goals. Accrediting agencies also would find her comments congruent with what they think ought to be attended to in this degree. The dean, however, must take the process one step further; that is, because such goals are deceptively broad, each must be translated into expected behaviors, skills or content that can be learned—and further, that such learning can be observed and documented in some way in order that the learning of the student can be seen, reflected upon, and *integrated* into an understanding of ministry. In other words, the dean must be clear as to where a student will be positioned within a school's ministerial curriculum so that particular hoped for outcomes might be expected to occur.

To reflect more specifically on these issues, let us take this pastor's goal number three, "facilitating small groups–task and process oriented." The dean and faculty would need to translate that goal into a task that can be readily assessed; for example, "the student will effectively lead a small group experience in a local church." This kind of thing can be observed, and can result in specific behaviors and learning(s) that actually can occur and be observed and critically reflected upon by both students and professors. Further, such specific expectations can be built into course-work. For example: "in this quarter, the curriculum offers a practicum in small group leadership that will educate each student so that the following outcomes can be observed . . ."

Such curricular frameworks can be expanded or contracted to include necessary course sequences, field education experiences, and specific seminars. It would not be difficult to imagine how the hoped for outcome noted above might also lead, for example, to a re-designed field education program that might be accompanied by required integrative workshops, seminars, or course offerings.

In similar fashion, Knox College in Toronto named a set of outcome expectations for its MDiv curriculum that includes "capacity for ministry—fostering theological reflection on, and capacity for, the practice of ministry in congregational, ecclesial and public contexts." They then broke this general outcome into specific goals that could be observed and measured as the student proceeded through the course of study on what Knox names as various "levels" (e.g., a single course, a given year, the program as a whole).[6]

In a case study prepared for a consultation on MDiv revision, representatives of Knox noted: "For the level of a single course, one faculty member designed a template syllabus that demonstrated the necessary detail as to course policies, assignments, and expectations and showed how outcomes taken from the theological/critical competencies can be incorporated into a course."

Such single courses often look at grading with an eye toward self-assessment. For example, one professor in another school devised the following:

Grade "A" reflects superior integration, including:

all those things listed in "b" and "c,"below;

the incorporation of class discussions, assigned readings, and demonstrated superior understanding in two critical instance reports;

a final paper demonstrating integration (using the Wesley Quadrillateral); and, incorporating parish committee observations from relevant class assignments.

Grade "B" reflects commendable progress:

in the parish assignment as the student is observed to be developing the team skills necessary for ecclesial work;

in the student's ability to enumerate in clear and useful ways the terms and concepts read and discussed in class.

This continues, but you get the idea.

Mapping learning outcomes throughout a curriculum

When a faculty comes to understand the linking of program learning goals with observable outcomes and with larger curricular structures as their collective responsibility and, subsequently, learning goals are connected to expected outcomes in every facet of the degree program, the question quickly moves to an assessment as to how well or poorly the curriculum we have serves to help us equip/educate/train those students entrusted to our care. For example, some schools have determined that program assessment is the sum total of how well each learning goal has been (or has not been) taught by the collective faculty. But arriving at this point means first having become aware that there is a learning pattern or "map" already residing within "our" curriculum.

Returning to materials produced at Knox College, we read:

More time consuming has been the process of enumerating the pattern of courses for the whole three-year curriculum. Faculty members have had to make the transition to thinking about the curriculum as a pattern of sequences of courses that build on each other and interact with each other as student learning progresses. Here, the integration produced by basing the curriculum on the learning model has become evident. In a 'lateral' sense, the defined competencies are addressed by teaching and learning across all courses in any year of curriculum, even though some courses will carry a heavier load in assessing certain skills and others in assessing types of knowledge. In a 'longitudinal' sense, the various sequences build on the learning of the earlier courses in the sequence, that is, continue to develop and assess the competencies inherent in the courses."

In whatever way learning goals become integrated across the curriculum, such progress becomes a map for students, as well as for faculty. Describing the three to five years of an

MDiv course of study suggests how each course and the overall sequence contributes to the expected learning outcomes of a curriculum. Program assessment naturally follows, as one is led to ask, "does our curriculum in its current shape function to help a student move towards the goals we have stated?" This, of course, assumes that the dean has led the faculty in articulating the domains of competence required for effective ministry in forms likely to be undertaken by graduates. Only then can a school fully understand the kind of curriculum needed to create leaders for ministry.

Put more positively, when deeply understood in this way, a "curriculum" becomes **the educational delivery system of a school**, and not fiefdoms of competing guilds.

Further, each faculty member is enabled to clearly articulate how (or if) their educational course, practica, or contextual experience contributes to the degree program's overarching learning objectives. In this regard, an accreditor will ask to see the learning objectives framing the MDiv degree program and will check progress made by faculty in creating or revising syllabi to include learning opportunities and tasks that lead to observable results in relation to specific outcomes of the program as a whole.

Curriculum content across schools

While no two seminaries have, or should have, identical learning objectives for the MDiv course of study, accreditors are agreed that each program offered by a school must reflect specific content areas. An accredited MDiv program must include specific content that educates each student about religious heritage, cultural context, personal and spiritual formation, and capacity for ministerial and public leadership. Schools would do well to look at their own MDiv learning objectives and to consider them in light of these expectations.

For example, if a school that prides itself on preparing "minister scholars" were to build a pie chart regarding such learning objectives, they might determine the following balance: Religious Heritage: 80%; Cultural Context: 5%; Personal and Spiritual Formation: 5%; and Capacity for Ministerial and Public Leadership: 10%.

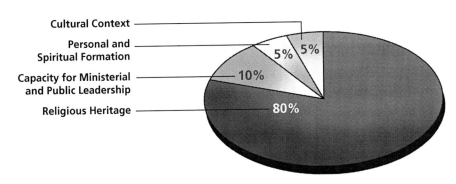

Another school that began as a school for laity and now prides itself as a place where practice is emphasized might have a different balance; for example, Religious Heritage: 40%; Cultural Context: 20%; Personal and Spiritual Formation: 10%; and Capacity for Ministerial and Public Leadership: 30%. While both pies "fit" the two schools' mission statements, one could easily distinguish one school's learning objectives from the other.

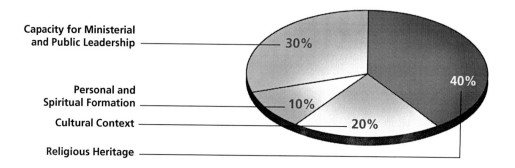

Making a pie chart like those above is one way faculty might begin to think intentionally about academic program assessment. It may help to structure faculty conversation in this area by noting that assessment of degree program is not the same thing as assessment of an individual student, and that the two must be considered separately, even as assessments of student learning should and must affect a faculty's understanding of the effectiveness of a specific degree and vice-versa.

Using such a visual chart with faculty can also introduce the sticky subject of integration. Integration often is a hidden or assumed goal of an MDiv curriculum, and a pie chart implicitly suggests a curricular wholeness, even when such wholeness does not exist. Academic Deans usually are more comfortable with visuals associating curriculum with a series of boxcars on a linear train track than with the image of a unified whole presented by a pie chart. However, they recognize that a linear curricular vision does not leave much room for integration, and, when pressed, often confess: "Frankly, we assume students will integrate the curriculum on their own." Nevertheless, integration of learning often is an expressed goal of a degree program, and usually is defined as a student being able to employ a variety of disciplines to a variety of issues that arise in a variety of contexts over time. Such integration of the learning goals of all aspects of the curriculum is not easy to achieve, or to measure. It is clear, however, that tools employed in the process of student assessment—notably, portfolios, initial seminars, team-taught courses, field education reflection seminars, and capstone courses—along with a general commitment to on-going and constructive student self-assessment, can contribute substantially to the attainment of integrative thinking on the part of most students by the time they complete their program of study.[7]

34

Perhaps, faculty, who hold doctoral degrees themselves, believe that the various integrative tools mentioned above are superfluous and that what students need is a final, integrative paper in which to demonstrate their best thinking, analogous to the PhD dissertation. However, I would argue, formation for ministry is only partially analogous to formation for success in the academy. So, while a cumulative MDiv project, such as a position paper, can indeed demonstrate a student's progress in integrative thinking, faculty need to think creatively about other types of integrative skills required for ministry, how to facilitate development of such skills, and how to assess when (and to what extent) students have achieved them.

A collective faculty vocation

While tension will always exist between the demands of the academy and the demands of the various institutions and contexts in which seminary graduates will do ministry, this book assumes that individuals who join a theological faculty are interested, at least to some degree, in educating students who have enrolled in pursuit of ministry education. That is, individual faculty members who want to help educate such persons for ministry and other forms of community leadership do not usually join a school that is devoted exclusively to PhD education. This book also assumes that a good faculty not only knows where it stands regarding this seminal issue, but also trusts each other enough to tackle those adjustments to the curriculum that inevitably come from program assessment. There will be needed changes; a static curriculum can become (very quickly) a dead curriculum. As a consequence, assessment and revision of the curriculum is best understood as the collective vocation of the faculty. In other words, in each particular school a unique group of persons is engaged in an on-going review and implementation of the educational delivery system occasioned by a particular vision and mission that brought them together in the first place.

That said, an accrediting committee will ask to see how a school (and the academic dean's office) regularly engages in assessment of each degree program offered by the school. Some schools do this with particular degree programs in, for example, an every-three-year review. Continuing with the example of the MDiv degree, a school that requires an integrative, senior position-in-ministry exam might evaluate, in such a review, how successful either a random or purposively chosen assortment of such position papers demonstrate how students attained, or failed to attain, the learning objectives of that course of study. Alternatively, a school might conduct focus interviews with bishops or area ministers regarding the effectiveness of their graduates in conjunction with the MDiv learning objectives. Still others might invite those who have served as "case conference leaders" in the field education program to visit the seminary for an "interpretive lunch" on the health of the MDiv program. And, still others might hire an outside consultant every three years to help the faculty assess the program, during an "in service" day or on retreat.

Many schools indicate that the level of such assessment conversations was elevated in their institutions with the appointment of degree program "directors." With such structural changes came a set of committees charged by the school to review not only the learning objectives of a given degree program with the full faculty, but to ask on a continual basis about ways each degree could better be structured to accomplish its stated objectives.

While curriculum decisions are often "turf" driven instead of "learning" driven, implementing the type of assessment procedures outlined above is one effective way to shift this dynamic. Looking carefully at how degree objectives are or are not accomplished usually moves a school further along the path toward a integrated and effective curriculum than the re-shuffling process that often occurs when this process is approached via the guild route.

The dean as department head

While the chief academic officer/academic dean is the person invested with the responsibility to ensure that student learning assessment is occurring and that assessment of the academic program takes place, the academic dean also has to shape the job descriptions and assessment procedures for the academic staff, including secretaries, student employees, deans of students, field education supervisors, registrars, chaplains, and directors of admissions.

In most of these cases, the academic dean tries to have in place an adequate job description, a clearly stated evaluation process, and a policy manual publicly detailing administrative concerns. For example, such a manual always outlines policies related to how people are paid, how sick leave is administered, and what happens in the case of allegation of sexual harassment. Such policy manuals often also contain historic agreements and are, therefore, the objects of close scrutiny by accreditation teams.

This is a complex terrain requiring good negotiating skills, but there also are some practices in every school that can move the school toward "win/win" accomplishments for both the dean and those whom the dean must assess, including faculty. For example, on the final day of class, students in many schools are asked to fill out evaluative instruments on the effectiveness of a professor's course. These forms are collected and frequently make their way into a professor's annual evaluative conversation with the dean. Some schools go so far as to weight these evaluations and to report the resulting statistics in comparative fashion for faculty merit pay increases. Such statistics, in conjunction with other evaluative materials, are often used in contract and tenure decisions. Upon closer scrutiny, what these practices seem to suggest is that, instead of the evaluation of a course, it is the individual professor who is being evaluated.

Were such instruments tied instead to the evaluation of the learning goals associated with the course, those goals and expected outcomes could be used to build course evaluation forms, thereby providing the faculty with useable data for critical reflection as to the present usefulness of the course and helping them understand the role it was intended to play in this particular degree. A Likert five-point scale could do this (rank on a scale of 1 to 5 with 1 being high agreement). Such a process shifts the responsibility for the revision of specific courses from each individual faculty member to a more corporate vision of ensuring that each course contributes appropriately to the overall goals of the curriculum.

Faculty evaluation

Accrediting visitors assume that the school will have an evaluation policy or procedure for faculty and a *Faculty Manual (or Handbook)* in place that, among other things, details certain aspects of faculty work-load policy, retention policy, promotion policy, and what steps **must** be taken for yearly, individual faculty evaluation and assessment. Schools approach this in a variety of ways, but every school realizes that a visiting accreditation committee will have read the school's faculty manual and will then ask faculty members how that written manual squares with actual practice.

At least one theological school employs a peer review process and faculty report it to be useful. A review committee meets every three and five years with individual professors. The person being reviewed outlines her or his "personal pedagogy," "goals for the future" and other accomplishments and commitments in a paper. The committee engages the professor in a conversation based on that paper, and then carefully makes a response based on its cumulative knowledge. A part of this response is to suggest how the individual might receive additional support from the institution. A deadline for a journal article's completion, a talk to be presented at a brown bag lunch, or a new team assignment for a course might be discussed. A teaching style change or try-out might draw a friendly coach from the committee, with the professor's agreement. Class observation and reflection might follow. But all such observations and comments occur outside the academic dean's formal annual faculty review.

Almost every school also follows a faculty evaluation procedure during which all individual faculty meet with the dean. A co-signed document usually emerges from this encounter. Some schools base their yearly "faculty review" conversations entirely on statements written by each faculty member and the academic dean prior to the meeting. Other schools add information from peer reviews, student course assessments, ordination exam area results, curriculum review committees, and faculty promotion reports. There appears to be no "right" way for doing faculty evaluation, but academic deans (and school lawyers) note that in matters of faculty review, the dean should follow the printed text of the *Faculty Manual* **without exception.** Accordingly, all schools indicate some form of yearly review with outlined procedures in the *Faculty Manual* that results in the annual addition of a co-signed document to each person's confidential faculty file.

What we have learned

Clearly, the academic dean has a lot to deal with in structuring and maintaining a variety of assessment processes. The dean is responsible for student learning assessment, and is also the head of a division in the school with its attendant personnel and policy documents. The accrediting committee will not only be interested in these items, but will also want to know how the school assesses its curriculum. These three concerns for assessment lie at the heart of what a dean "does"; that is, the dean helps facilitate a faculty's better understanding of its common vocation in service to the mission of the school.

CHAPTER 4

ASSESSING THE REMAINING INSTITUTIONAL DEPARTMENTS: THE PRESIDENT'S OFFICE

"The ideal candidate for president of this institution will have outstanding experience in educational management, demonstrated ability to inspire and to lead the academic community, demonstrated ability to link the school with its constituencies, the capacity to work effectively and credibly with the board of trustees, a record of successful implementation of strategic initiatives, a demonstrated capacity for planning and budgeting, a demonstrated ability to manage fiscal resources effectively, an open, collaborative leadership style, and a demonstrated commitment to participatory governance."

A posting in relation to a Presidential search in The Chronicle of Higher Education[8]

Not all schools approach assessment as a *team*. Some university divinity school deans and schools closely intertwined with colleges have access to university/ college personnel who include the school in the university or college assessment system. A few presidents have sufficient numbers of students that they can hire enough dedicated personnel to staff an assessment office. Other presidents simply drop "the assessment chore" on the academic dean's desk. Others appoint a "task force/standing committee" charged with developing and then monitoring the school's assessment program. Still others look to someone inside or outside the school who has expertise in this area and who can assume overall responsibility for assessment. All of these approaches can work more or less well, depending on intangibles such as how the faculty and administrators respond when they are informed how assessment will occur at "their" school.

The fact remains that, as far as accrediting bodies are concerned, the point person on institutional assessment in a theological school is the president (or, in Canada, the principal; or in university settings, the divinity school dean). While the president is not alone in this endeavor, it is the president to whom the accreditation committee turns when asking about purpose, planning, and evaluation. Accordingly, this chapter considers the role of the president in the assessment process. Of course, presidents must rely on other officers, so we must consider not only the individual who is President, but her team as well, "The President's Office."

Because context and personality are such critical factors in seminaries where among other things strong faculties are common, the implementation of an effective assessment structure and process is a moment where the leadership "style" of the president can be seen to either work or fail.

Presidential leadership styles

Presidents lead in different ways. One way is primarily **hierarchical** in nature. Hierarchical leadership is when the president and/or the president's cabinet serve as primary interpreters of the data, naming the issues and deciding what strategies and tactics to implement. A second, **consultative** style is not quite so "top down" but a "the buck stops with me" presidential authority remains. In consultative mode, the president/cabinet ask for input from other persons and groups outside their own group, but retain the main decision-making and interpretive process about the meaning of data and the choice of strategies to follow.

A third way, the **interactive**, is much more "horizontal" in character. An interactive leader will create assessment/planning processes that are fully participatory in the sense that data are interpreted by the persons who have the best knowledge and judgment about the data. Decisions in such a process are also made at appropriate levels, especially with the participation of those who must implement the decisions. This does not mean that the president is uninvolved or simply embraces a laissez faire style, but is the person or office that sets up, manages, and controls the whole assessment/planning process while pushing to see that it is carried out in a timely and effective manner at all levels of the institution.

For example, assuming an interactive approach, the president might seek focused conversations on a strategic issue involving a wide variety of people from the governing board, the faculty, and other interior and exterior constituencies. By doing so, the president assumes a decision can be reached at appropriate governance levels by those most closely involved and takes responsibility to see that this happens and that the decision is, in turn, assessed once implemented.

Is one style better?

Most seminary presidents use one of these three styles most of the time. Some presidents are very explicit in naming how they will proceed to make decisions on a daily basis; others see the three styles as options to be used largely determined by contextual circumstances. They know that as the school itself changes over time, so too must the president make adaptive changes to their leadership style. Such presidents suggest that the key to becoming a good president is knowing when to use which style. That decision depends a lot on what the issue is, timing, urgency, who is accountable, who is designated and responsible for a particular area, and who has the authority to take action. The hard part of this "mix and/or match" process is knowing when and how to use each style.

In the current era, presidents in higher education must also understand and embrace the promotion of an "assessment culture." Such an initiative assumes a broad base of persons in the institution actively committed to the assessment/planning process. Presidents need to ask themselves how their leadership style either enables or blocks such understanding in their school.

All three styles have pluses and minuses; no one is necessarily better or worse than another one. The "top-down" model (hierarchical) clarifies authority and, when assessment issues need declarative action, provides a ready solution. Unless support staff understand (and accept) their roles however, passive-aggressive behavior (and sometimes more explicit resistance) will occur.

The second (consultative) position may appear, at first glance, to avoid resentment that can turn into resistance, but it too has its risks. Asking for input from many, may encourage "Monday-morning quarterbacks" to say, "It would have gone better if only the president had listened to my advice." The plus side of the consultative position is that when the assessment discussion is a good one, multiple sides of the issue get exposed and resistance is less likely.

While the third posture (interactive) is almost one of consensus, not many presidents will keep discussion open until all parties come to full agreement. This third stance, however, is more horizontal and open, and should encourage more assessment "buy-in" on the part of others. This stance also takes time and deliberately presents assessment issues as peer issues to be discussed. On occasion, a president may need to act with more speed than this model permits.

Some presidents will be able to accomplish the task of getting an institutional "team" assessment structure in place by utilizing a hierarchical style of leadership. Others will succeed at establishing the processes needed through a consultative approach, even though they employ a more horizontal, interactive style in other aspects of their leadership role. Still others will use the interactive approach as institutional assessment issues arise and are addressed through collaborative processes.

The institutional departmental structure: the team's context

Understanding presidential leadership styles, knowing when and how to use one style rather than another, and building a team that does assessment within the context of a specific school is not an easy task. It may be easier to conceive what is at stake in bringing life to a school's institutional assessment process, if we set aside the particular histories, tensions and gift of our particular institutions and reflect for a moment more generically.

Let's say, for instance, we were building a brand new theological school. This gives us the opportunity to interweave assessment procedures throughout the entire institutional structure. In order to fully understand what this would look like, we'd ask first, "What departments or divisions are necessary in order for the school to achieve its mission?" A generic answer might give us a structure composed of the academic, business, development, and student services departments.

Second, we might then ask, "What mission-connected tasks are central to each of these departments?" For example, the academic dean and the school's faculty might see as their central task "the development and maintenance of an educational delivery system (curriculum, degree programs, faculty, library, etc.)." Likewise, other departments might name tasks appropriate to their departments. For example, the development office might suggest that its central role is "to build a relational matrix of friends, constituencies, and agencies supportive of the school, and to provide the school with a developmental plan and a case that would be used in the raising of resources sufficient to carry the school into the next century." All of the remaining departments in the school would be asked to fashion similar mission-based tasks for their departments.

Third, each department would be asked to put into place manuals or handbooks summarizing the assessment processes and procedures that are central to the department, including job descriptions and how annual reviews occur for all personnel. This kind of evaluative assessment is usually straightforward. Personnel would be evaluated on a yearly basis and handbooks would be evaluated every three to five years, or as the need arises. (While some might argue that such "administrative tasks" are not *really* assessment tasks, those who don't regularly attend to such evaluative, administrative procedures can find themselves in deep trouble when policies become outdated and, thus, inappropriate when trying to do formal assessment, since data will be lacking. Accordingly, accreditation committees pay particular attention to manuals and procedural policies as examples of good, or bad, "planning.")

Envisioning institutional assessment

If we had the luxury of designing a new school with departments organized around key mission-based tasks and with departmental assessment processes appropriately in place, then we could also begin to envision what *institutional assessment* might look like.

For example, given this new school's organizational structure, a perfectly legitimate institutional assessment question can be asked by the president: "Given department X, does the school currently have the necessary human, physical, and financial resources in place needed to accomplish its mission-related tasks? If not, then what needs to occur in order that the necessary resources are in place? And, what priorities must be altered, advanced, or dropped?"

Accordingly, this assessment process unfolds both within and across departmental structures. The president can expect each department to clarify its question in light of "good practice" even as it moves to gather relevant data, interprets that data, and carries initial proposals into the president's council. In that venue, adjustments are made to each proposal, and appropriate determinations reached as to their viability. A few are quickly implemented; others—perhaps with more at stake— are sent into the relevant governance structures for further deliberation.

The president has responsibility for putting into place the constructive building blocks of this ongoing institutional assessment structure, chief among them being the identification of competent administrators and getting them "on the bus." Accordingly, administrators are chosen because they can do the job, understand the relevance of mission in this setting, and are team players. Getting such a team in place is an absolutely critical step. Once in place, the team must regularly meet with the president; this goes beyond simply calling this group a "leadership team." It is within this setting that institutional data is collected from the departments and decisions are made for the school.

Paying attention to context: using the audit

Once such a team is functioning, it is the president who puts assessment at the heart of the new enterprise. Since this is a new school, its context, both internally and externally, must be continually assessed in order that it become effective in both day-to-day institutional assessment and strategic planning.

While few presidents have the luxury of putting a totally new administrative structure into place, the president always determines to what extent the assessment process is regularly implemented within each department or division of the school. In this regard, good leadership teams will meet, and interior and exterior audits will become primary tools that help both the school and the president better understand the tasks that lie ahead of them.

Some would say that regular **audits** of the interior/exterior context of the school are the primary tools for dealing with change. They would also argue that rapid change is inevitable for all institutions and that no final control can be perfectly exercised in any planning procedure, no matter how such audits are designed or carried out. They also believe, however, that this is no excuse for not carefully monitoring the institution's vision and mission in light of its interior/exterior context. They would suggest that the regular use of various audits effectively guards the institution against unpleasant surprises.

For example, an *internal audit* assesses several factors—what for example, strongly positions the school? Are these *human* factors? For example, perhaps the school employs a first-rate administrative team that is imaginative and trustworthy. Perhaps the school also has a faculty deeply committed to the school's mission. All well and good, but are there other strengths that are composed of *physical* factors? Perhaps the school is growing and current buildings are in good shape and there is ample land for expansion. Or, are there positive *financial* factors? Perhaps the school has a balanced budget and a diversified constituency that financially supports the school while an endowment has been enabled to grow.

The flip side is that such audits can also expose a school's weaknesses—for example, the internal audit might note that while the school has a good faculty (human factors), perhaps several key players will retire over the next five years. And, while the current buildings (physical factors) are in good shape, perhaps the school understands that it is gradually moving from a residential population into a new non-residential educational model that, while not yet fully understood, might eventually find the current residential housing to be an albatross. Perhaps, as well, the school is too smug regarding its healthy financial picture (financial factors). That smugness may be shattered with the realization that two of the key trustees who have helped position the school in the financial sector are retiring from the board and are, at the same time, the only trustees who fully understand the negative market pressures on the school's endowment.

An *exterior audit* will attempt the same sort of analysis, starting with the local, regional, and national picture. In what ways can someone honestly depict the schools position in each terrain? The school can look at this question through a variety of lenses. For example, one lens is recruitment—perhaps a school's student base is changing. Perhaps a school understands itself as denominationally tied to one tradition, while the students in classes actually represent something else—an ever-expanding array of denominations. What might such change mean for the school—is it a crisis or an opportunity?

In similar fashion, a *constituency audit* seeks to develop a picture of real and potential supporters and friends of the school. Such an audit unpacks both the longitudinal implications of past constituency support and the changing face of such constituencies. It may also suggest that the present student population can help in this regard. Charts and graphs often are used to visualize the constituency or potential stakeholder ties of students. In addition, discovering where graduates go for employment sometimes uncovers still more

44

unrecognized constituencies. "Finding" such new friends often surprises those who assume that the configuration of the seminary's friends and constituencies is dependable (perhaps, static) over long periods of time.

The good president is always interested in having a regular audit of the *school's missional congruency* as well. This audit might begin by asking if the courses of study offered by the school are congruent with the stated intent of the school's mission statement. The president knows that such audit data must be presented for consideration and interpretation to both the faculty and the trustees.

Such audits, coupled with the annual *financial audit*, provide snapshots of what is going on while indicating possible trajectories that are either healthy or unhealthy for the school. The four-step assessment loop again comes into play, and strongly emphasizes the need for collecting data such as this and wrestling with it in order to consider what strategic initiatives make sense and should be implemented. "Making sense" has a lot to do with understanding how an emergent strategy connects with "our" current strengths and fits "our" mission, values, and vision.

While we have been speaking of presidential responsibilities thus far in this chapter, it is worth noting briefly, that at every stage of his process, the chief financial officer will be raising one question: How is the strategy we are talking about financially viable? Without this sober question, many schools add on programs or embark on initiatives that either slowly die from lack of resources or draw resources from other core elements of the instution, thereby hurting the school's overall financial health, because they have been built without a substantive answer to this question.

Cultivating assessment across departments

In institutional assessment, the president puts the mission into dialogue with the current context of the institution, continually directing missionally based questions into the assessment "loop," while regularly connecting departmental insights and perspectives into the decision-making process.

For example, the president might press particular departments into the assessment loop by posing questions like the following:
. . . to the *development director*: "Can you provide to the council a map of all our constituencies by September, and can you direct a conversation with the council that might help us interpret your map and develop proposals that might structure development (relational) work over the next three years?"
. . . to the *student services director*: "Can you provide the council with a longitudinal study

of our student population by November, commencing with fifteen years ago, coupling that data with other data from academic program enrollment and denominational and national religious data, and then lead a conversation in council regarding that data and several proposals generated by your department?"

. . . to the *chief financial officer*: "In January, I would like you to work with the development officer and the student services officer as they produce possible scenarios from their departments. Run several of their ideas through your financial modeling process. Try to see how they work independently, in tandem with each other, and perhaps how they work if "we" have distinctive academic populations that are either similar or different than what exists now. When we push each financial model's parameters, do they suggest new institutional priorities?"

When the president intentionally utilizes the council venue as a primary crossroad for such work, given the resulting data and proposal generation, the school begins to understand (in a useful way) what assessment "experts" call an effective "culture of assessment." The drive toward institutional learning by realizing such a culture of assessment begins within the office of the president.

The office of the president

This chapter initially touched on presidential leadership style, suggesting that presidents either learn to lead by relying on the integrity of the departmental structure (and those heading such departments), or sink under the weight of trying to "do" too much of what necessarily must take place.

In this regard, presidents need to know that at one point in the history of higher education a president pretty much ran the entire enterprise. He (and I employ the male gender intentionally) not only enrolled the students and raised the money to finance things, but also was a gifted scholar, a pastor/mentor to every student, and an occasional janitor. As times changed, the president began to have a more focused external role, and the academic dean's position was invented for interior work with curriculum, students, and faculty concerns. But the dean's role also changed. With further complications rooted in increasing professionalism and specialization, schools began to hire persons to deal exclusively, for example, with finances or with students. No longer would the academic dean function as admission's officer, registrar, and bursar! And now schools have added technology personnel to deal with that revolution as well.

Today the good development officer nurtures the school's relational donor base while accompanying the president on targeted visits. And it is the good president who spends as much as sixty percent of the workweek on such visits.

The "office of the president", therefore, can't run on style alone; there must be many, trusted players on the team. Presidents must rely on administrative secretaries, operational managers, and an increasing cohort of other officers who together constitute "the office of the president," or the core leadership team. Competence, collegiality, and a shared commitment to the missional objectives of the school are the cardinal virtues required of each member of this core group.

I've named some of the assessment concerns that must be faced by the competent academic dean in Chapter Three; here, I continue that conversation by suggesting some of the ways several other key officers contribute to the work of overall institutional assessment that is the responsibility of the office of the president.

The business department and the CFO

The chief financial officer (CFO) has primary responsibility for the budget. Good CFOs not only have transparent budget reporting systems with monthly actuals and accurate numbers, but they also have the ability to do financial modeling. In other words, they can introduce specific changes into their financial budgets and then make projections over time as to how such changes might affect the budget (and the bottom line).

Financial modeling occurs whenever a financial officer is asked to develop a number of models or scenarios based on adjustments that would need to be made if one of a number of strategies under consideration is chosen and implemented. For example, one school wanted to both increase tuition revenue and encourage increased use of central campus facilities. The financial officer experimented with a number of models and then ran a counter-intuitive model that suggested such goals might be reachable by lowering the tuition rate for full-time students in a particular degree program. The school tried this idea. The discount turned out to be very attractive to a number of part-time students and enough took advantage of it so that the discount model "worked"—more tuition revenue was raised than had been raised in previous years and housing, cafeteria, and other central campus revenue also experienced favorable gains.

Because the discount rate applied to a single program, the CFO could watch it over time. Whether or not this particular model would work in other programs (or schools) would be dependent on a number of particular variables, but such intentionality is suggestive. Financial modeling can be a useful planning tool in fine-tuning institutional planning initiatives. It is crucial in managing risk factors and fears when a new initiative is put into practice.

All administrators, in some fashion, are directly influenced by what gets into (or is held out of) the budget. In one sense, *the budget* is a school's central document emerging from the consolidation of a school's institutional assessment process. As such, the budget becomes a political/missional document that consumes a good deal of planning/assessment conversation in the president's cabinet. This document, in other words, distributes the resources according to the values inherent in the mission of the school, but not only this. The budget also reflects the ongoing strategic decisions that are emerging from the assessment and planning conversation held in the president's cabinet. The CFO often is at the center of this conversation.

At the same time, the CFO has responsibility for other subsidiary evaluation/assessment procedures. For example, a *building audit* might provide important information about deferred maintenance or the priorities of a capital funds campaign. Whether or not such an audit exists, the visiting accrediting committee may ask the CFO if any money has been regularly set aside for deferred maintenance (for example, annually setting aside 2% of the assessed value of the physical plant in a "rainy day" fund). If no funds are currently being set aside, that same committee may also ask what financial model led the school not to have a deferred maintenance line item in the budget.

While such systemic questions are critical to assessing the on-going financial health of a school, the *annual audit* can also be understood to be a useful evaluation tool regarding a school's health. The audit includes a letter addressing marginal or inadequate financial practice(s). If the school regularly folds this letter's data into the interpretation/proposal/decision-making steps (the assessment loop), then inadequate financial practices will be addressed. In one sense, how the school (and the CFO) deal with the annual audit provides the visiting accreditation committee with a snapshot as to the relative health of the school's assessment/planning process.

It is important to note in this regard that the accreditation visitor will ask the CFO how the budget is built, how the audit information is used, how employees in this office understand their jobs, and if an employee manual exists. These questions serve as a way to engage the CFO regarding not only the relative health of the school, but also the procedures followed in this department that are connected to the school's assessment plan.

The development department and the development officer

Too often development officers are only tangentially related to the school's assessment process. This, despite the fact that development officers have almost daily contact with constituencies *outside* the school. Because the development officer was hired to build relationships and raise money, the school that actively pursues assessment will intentionally benefit from the data that can be gained from this person's broad and regular interactions.

To contribute efficiently and substantially to institutional assessment, the development officer should regularly host conversations with members of specifically chosen constituent groups about the seminary's mission. Such groups, either connecting at this meeting for the first and only time or reconnecting as the result of a long-standing role played with the seminary, could offer invaluable data as to how the school and its mission are perceived. Such focus group conversations are a primary tool that capital fund consultants use in order to determine perceptions as to the clarity of the school's mission and whether or not members of the focus group would give money to the school to enable it to fulfill that mission.

Nevertheless, schools regularly dismiss comments about how the "mission" is perceived by various constituents from the development officer. These are often perceived to be the idiosyncratic musings of the officer and rarely serve as an interpretive location for sorting new data about the perception of the school "out there." Perhaps this has to do with the lack of an assessment plan that includes gathering data through the development office from constituents in a regularized fashion. If the development officer were charged with producing a *Focus Review of the School's Mission* every two or three years, for example, such data could be interpreted by a standing committee, which in turn could develop proposals and initiate important conversations at the cabinet level.

In this regard, some schools understand the development officer as a trusted relational window to various constituencies, including alumni/ae. Such places, as they move into a more comprehensive assessment program, increasingly look to the development officer to help them monitor how the institution is perceived by alumni/ae and other important, outside constituencies. It is crucial to cultivate, throughout the institution, an understanding of the development officer as relationally based, instead of just financially based.

Development, however, is an office and an administrative area (or unit) like every other department in the school. Accordingly, accrediting committees will ask how many dollars are spent through this office in order to raise how many dollars. They will also ask how the development officer understands and has come to build the school's "case" for development purposes and how that case ties into the school's mission. In addition, they will ask if the employees in the development office have job descriptions, annual reviews, and access to an employee manual detailing issues pertinent to their employment (including the employee policy on sexual harassment). These things will be raised not only as part of the visitors' questions about what the development office does for the school, but how assessment helps the development office do its job better.

The student personnel officer and office

Like all of the officers noted above, the student personnel officer must also be concerned with job descriptions, a policy manual, and the holding of annual personnel reviews.

Persons charged with working with students (recruiters, admissions officers, financial officers, deans of students, deans of chapel, spiritual directors, registrars, etc.) are the glue that hold the school together on a daily basis. These are the faces that interpret school policies on such things as late payments and whether or not a student's pet is allowed in seminary housing. Nevertheless, many schools do not include someone on the president's cabinet to represent this area.

In any event, student personnel officers who understand and bring into play the dynamics associated with *student enrollment management* should be at the center of the assessment process in a given school. Much like the CFO who has mastered the intricacies of *financial modeling*, the student personnel officer who understands the interconnectedness of recruitment, curriculum, retention, placement, and the ongoing support/rejection by alumni/ae can ask the right assessment questions. For example, one school tracked how entering students had initially connected with the school. While the school's recruitment office had spent much of their budget on print materials oriented to attract younger students, only one of the entering students in that age category recalled those materials as being particularly effective. Seven other students in that age category, however, were quite clear that their initial connection with the school was via the school's website (which had used some, but not all, of the youth-oriented graphics). But ahead of the website and ranking highest as far as "initial connection" were another eight persons who noted that "graduates or friends of the seminary" initially introduced them to the school. Such data must be mined carefully, but one clear conclusion was if this age category was to be vigorously reached, both the school's website and an intentional "connections" program (that worked with graduates and friends of the school) would need regular attention.

But getting students *into* a theological school is only a part of what student enrollment management entails. For example, what is your school's retention rate and how many years does it take for someone to graduate from each of your school's degree programs? Keeping and graduating people in a timely fashion is important, both for morale and for bottom line considerations. Student enrollment managers accordingly seek lots of assessment data and should attend to all four steps in the assessment "loop." In this regard, some schools organize student personnel into *teams* charged to sort their impressions, gather data, make proposals, and implement some of the decisions that are made. Such teams often reside under the office and personal guidance of the academic dean. Others have a specific structure that places someone like the dean of students as the "chair" of the student personnel team. Still other schools are of such a size that a larger structure with interlocking areas of student personnel responsibility reside under the authority of someone with a title such as "vice president of student affairs." Often such persons are accorded a seat on the leadership team.

Whatever structures are in place, directives regarding evaluation/assessment of student perceptions and concerns about the school and its program will fall into this area. For example, one school reported initially hiring a consultant who crafted a "hospitality" survey that, once completed, became the basis of a committee survey done (with the committee itself reworking specific parts of the survey for future surveys) every three years. Another school annually "rates" how students feel about student personnel procedures via conversations held during free "pizza lunches." Each lunch is composed of an intentionally chosen group of students who are asked a series of questions about a particular set of concerns. Data are recorded, transcribed, and fed back into the student affairs committee for its consideration. Another school provides a "community bulletin board" on its webpage; every month one staff member poses a question on the bulletin board and then prints the responses. So far, this process has enabled the leadership team to identify several key student issues.

Schools that regularly seek data through such collection devices report that their data are very useful in their weekly "team" meeting. They sort the data and ask themselves how best they can address what they call "real" concerns. This exercise has helped bring them together across their areas of responsibility and encouraged them to work together as a team to address such issues.

The accreditation visitor will have a series of questions for those who work in this area. These questions may range from "are all credentials and student records adequately secured?" to "how do students understand the sexual harassment policy?" That this area is a unit with job descriptions, policy manuals for school employees (and for students), and evaluation procedures in place will also need to be demonstrated to accreditation visitors.

What we have learned

Five administrators often comprise the core of what gets called the office of the president: 1) the academic dean; 2) the chief financial officer; 3) the development officer; 4) the student personnel officer; and 5) the president.

It is the *president* who has the primary responsibility for developing and relying on this team, in order to accomplish the missional objectives of the school. To the degree that an assessment plan is in place, it becomes operationally effective through these persons. The office of the president is the place where concerns will surface, data will be discussed, and strategies deployed. It is here that departmental issues move into and through institutional structures and are changed, via interpretive conversations, into legitimate institutional initiatives that are then presented at the board level. When only bits and pieces of interpretative data related to a set of concerns surface at the council level, it is also the responsibility of council members to clarify the issues, gather more data, and continue discussing options. This can become chaotic unless someone keeps track of all the balls that are in the air. Keeping track is perhaps the primary, on-going responsibility of the president.

The president needs to honor all the various proposals that departments submit, while keeping in mind an overall, systemic meta-sense regarding the institutions resources and intended goals—and, of course, the ways in which all of this related to the mission of the school. This is a bit like cooking a good meal—one must attend to the whole while also being aware of what happens to each of the component parts. So, for instance, while it is good to have someone fetch the apples from the farmer's market and another to peel and chop them, the chef wants on this day to get the apples between the pie crusts to make the desired dessert, not thrown into the stew pot (unless, of course, the stew is mulligatawny, and calls for apples).

When an accreditation visitor asks to see the school's overall assessment plan, he or she expects a narrative from the president and the other key players detailing how this particular school understands and addresses assessment. The visitor would also expect to see evidence of the successful completion of several cycles of that plan.

The responsibility for such concerns lies squarely on the president's desk While the president also carries special responsibility for the completion of assessment procedures related to board structure, board members, administrative positions, and the office of the president, other administrators are charged by the president to assess the areas that they administer. Nevertheless, the president, as chief administrator, must facilitate assessment despite the way various structures, personalities, and the process itself may generate resistances. The "buck" stops on the president's desk. Therefore, while the president can choose from among the different leadership "styles" the one that might be most effective, in the end, it is getting assessment done that counts.

CHAPTER 5

ASSESSING INSTITUTIONAL GOVERNANCE: THE BOARD OF DIRECTORS

---

*A model of shared governance empowers a
school to draw on the wisdom and experience
of all while also, as much as possible, assuring
a high degree of ownership of the actions that are
taken to respond to various changes.*

Gordon T. Smith[9]

How does assessment connect with the issue of governance in a theological school? Robert Cooley defines **governance** as "the self-correcting system we design, build, and maintain to balance the legitimate interests of policy-making and decision-making structures toward fulfillment of the seminary's mission and sustained economic vitality." He continues: "Shared governance includes collaboration, information gathering, interpretation and decision-making."[10]

Much of this definition is congruent with the definition of **assessment** that is detailed in this book. This connection is better understood through a closer look at governance and the governing board.

Governance

The effectiveness of governance in theological education depends upon the necessary distance that exists between the governing board and the faculty, or academic council. Trustees tend to see the big picture (i.e., how the school is situated in the larger economic, social and ecclesial context) while faculty tend to concentrate on the school's educational delivery system. Both concerns are relevant to the school's defining and reaching missional objectives, but **authority** in relation to each body must be clearly defined in policy-setting documents in order to ensure that the deployment of authority is constructive rather than destructive.

The president and the office of the president stands between the governing board and the academic council. Good presidents use the energy associated with this posture to affirm the legal responsibilities of trustees and the professional responsibilities of faculty, while constructing and implementing a system-wide, decision-making assessment process through which the seminary begins to realize its missional objectives. What happens in the president's office accordingly is of deep interest to both faculty and trustees.

The office of the president

Shared governance occurs when the decision-making assessment process based in the office of the president is connected with appropriate parties through an information-producing system that directs relevant information from across the institution to the board. As such, the process that unfolds within this office affects seminary culture as well as the likelihood that a school will accomplish its missional objectives.

A small institution will approach the president's office and those who comprise the president's cabinet with an intimate, collegial understanding of governance and the shared tasks that they must address. The larger an institution becomes, the more bureaucratic it also inevitably becomes. And bureaucracy tends to encourage hierarchy. Still, even in rigid hierarchy, good governance and good decision-making remain shared tasks because those close to the ground have the data that those at the top need to proceed. Both small and large institutions should engage in the construction and maintenance of a shared governance system that provides effective, collegial decision-making for the institution. Accreditation visitors will stress the "shared" aspect of this process as central to "good" governance and "good" assessment procedures.

Three types of institutions

Even in the cozy world of graduate theological education, shared governance looks different in different contexts. Some schools are free-standing, and can construct governance in whatever way they choose. Others, connected to a college or university, are embedded within the governance and decision-making processes of those entities. Still others have ecclesiastical relationships that shape, or even determine, their governance structures. In such situations, the school's autonomy can range from relative independence from church authorities to substantial control by them. At the same time, all three types necessarily delegate at least enough authority to administrators and faculty to go about their designated professional responsibilities. While the way decisions are made differs among these three types, whether governance and decision-making processes work (or do not work) is fundamentally dependent upon whether a bond of trust is experienced (or not experienced) between the school and its central staff members (i.e., the officers and faculty) and the board of trustees, university governors or ecclesiastical authorities.

Good and bad governance

There is no guarantee that governance, even when perfectly structured according to the best available model, will therefore always be "good." Accordingly, there are always examples of "bad" governance. For example, good governance practice asserts that boards should always interact with the school as a board, but schools often report that individual board members attempt to micro-manage the internal seminary decision-making processes. Schools then experience bad governance.

On other occasions, well-drawn governance structures fail in the midst of actual practice or unexpected crises. For example, if good governance practice suggests that presidents should have avenues for input early in tenure discussions, the absence of a clearly drawn process that allows such early input can lead to a governance crisis when the president (late in the game) rejects a committee's recommendation regarding a professor's tenure status. Again, bad governance occurs.

But there also can be good governance. For example, when a school's system of governance has been carefully documented and has survived a sudden shift in central personnel, such as the unexpected departure of a president, intact, then governance has been successful. Even if the transition period was not as smooth as one could hope, such a result can be said to represent good governance. Good governance accordingly implies the presence of an institutionally accepted system of governance built on trust and discovered to be useful in practice.

Interestingly enough, every school with which I am familiar asserts that it has, in fact, a good system of governance and assessment in place. No two schools, however, approach either shared governance or assessment in the same way. The ethos/culture of the school and its constituencies and religious tradition(s) come into play on both accounts. The personalities that make up the board, faculty, and office of the president also enter into these equations. Nevertheless, despite all these potential (and substantive) sources of tension, the objective of every theological institution is to realize missional objectives while maintaining economic vitality. One way such occurs is through a blend of good assessment and good governance.

Assessment is interwoven with governance

Assessment is the ongoing system of mechanisms that regularly produce data that faculty, staff and trustees can interpret and use in helpful ways to make decisions about policies and initiatives that will enable the school to accomplish its mission. Such data, along with various interpretations, regularly appear on the docket of a duly authorized venue, often the president's cabinet, where interpretations get sorted out and decision-making takes place. When the system is working well, few decisions need to be passed on to other bodies, freeing the board of trustees to consider the "big picture" that is its mandate, and the academic council, the delivery of quality education to the students.

Assessment can be understood as that decision-making, shared governance process unfolding under the guidance of the president and the governing board. Linkages to various interior/exterior committees, task forces, departments, and governance venues (like the board and the academic council) provide appropriate routes for information sharing and proposal dissemination. The critical central location in this system remains the president's office.

Controlling data flow: dashboard reports

In the president's cabinet, the assessment process makes use of those data already readily available to the school from sources outside of the school.[11] At the same time, the departments or working teams are asked to provide information about their respective internal areas in the form of four or five key indicators that must be monitored in real time in order that the school understand its strengths and weaknesses. The defining of such key indicators is absolutely critical to the flow of useful data into the appropriate governance venues. Nowhere is the phrase "garbage in, garbage out" more appropriate.

A finance committee and a chief financial officer might suggest that one such key indicator is the school's data regarding endowment draw-down as it connects with the current state of its annual campaign. Other useful numbers might be the current head count of the student body and the number of credit hours billed in the current semester. These indicators might be viewed by the school over a four-year time span, thus defining positive or negative trajectories.

Another committee headed by a senior faculty member and charged with the responsibility for the admission process of the school might provide data from recruitment, including the applicant pool, their ages, diversity, gender, and denominational background. Beyond these, the number of contacts made with potential applicants, projections based on past performance, and other indicators that might impact the need for scholarship support in relation to expected billable hours could be quite helpful. These indicators might also be pursued longitudinally.

Still another committee, occasioned by work done through the development office, might report narrative data collected from a series of conversations with focus groups made up of graduates from ten and fifteen years ago, respectively, who were asked to describe how well the school prepared them to succeed in their various careers and to list issues that they currently face in their vocations. If such interviews are regularized in format, such data can become significant over time.

Such information is then collated and provided in summary form to the president's cabinet. This group interacts with the data. Having decided what data is pertinent to governance decision-making, they forward these statistics to the governing board, whether in raw or summary form. Secure web-sites now make it possible for a president's council, should it so choose, to make such data more accessible to others, as well.

As this information is presented to the governing board, many schools format it as a "dashboard" report. **Dashboard reports**[12] take key indicators as defined by an institution and reduce those data to an easily read one to three page report that makes such information transparent and accessible to the reader. Schools can, thereby, report complex data via simplified key indicator graphics that also illustrate trajectories. Information of a narrative sort (as from the focus groups above) can also be reduced to several emergent themes and reported within a single sheet addition to the dashboard.

An example of dashboard categories follows. Note that most of the items can be displayed as ratios, percentages, or simple numbers. The two categories marked with an asterisk might be more helpfully presented in the form of simple narratives. An interpretive hermeneutic can be developed by the president as this data is presented to the board.

Students
1. # inquires/# matriculated
2. % yield/% retention
3. FTE #/HC #
4. Full demographic picture
5. Debt load #s
6. Dollars spent/return ratio

Finances
1. Monthly budget actuals
2. # gifts received/gift ranges
3. Endowment position/draw-down %
4. Annual fund actuals/% increase (decrease)
5. New donors located/donor demographic picture
6. Dollars spent/retention ratio

Educational Program
1. # faculty/student-faculty ratio
2. Workload distribution #s
3. Peer compensation comparisons
4. Program demographics
5. Exit survey data
*6. # who stay the course (in ministry survey one, five, ten years)

Board
1. General board demographic
2. # active board members/talent inventory
3. Board "get or give" #s
4. Evaluation data; president/administrators/ board members/board Structure and meetings
*5. Progress made on specific board initiatives
6. Policy inventory to date

This type of user-friendly data in an atmosphere of good governance often results in positive board action. Taking the time and developing the skills to turn raw statistics into transparent data also occasions higher morale throughout the institution and a positive sense of forward movement toward missional objectives.

Board assessment

In addition to good data control and exemplary work within departments and the president's council, other "good practices" can contribute significantly to the overall health of the institution. Assessment of the board itself is one such opportunity—and when carefully done can not only yield good data but can also communicate important and positive messages on a symbolic level.[13]

Assessment of the board is an opportunity for the board to consider how well it is doing its job. Some presidents formalize this question ("How well have we done this year as a board?") in a closed-session discussion at the end of each year. A discussion format inevitably leads to proposals for how the board might do better. The boards that intentionally pursue this assessment strategy suggest that a board-only executive session allows them to consider with the president not only their structure as a board, but also some intangibles—such as, for example, how they perceive the seminary institutional assessment system and the usefulness of the data that are regularly presented as the result of such procedures. Schools also note that in order to process issues that are raised, they have put in place a committee charged with devising ways to consider any proposals that might emerge from such conversations. As a suggestion, such proposals might be appropriately placed on a single-day fall or winter retreat agenda.

Assessing the president

Boards often have a personnel committee charged with the responsibility of annually assessing the president. While no two boards approach this crucial task in precisely the same fashion, most start by conducting focus conversations with key administrators and requesting a written self-evaluation report from the president. The committee reviews these data and produces a written document summarizing how the president is doing and what areas they want to reflect on with the president in person. This paper and the president's response to the initial written report then become the focus of a private meeting. Such meetings are, almost invariably, described by presidents as "anxiety producing, but invaluable." The results of such a review are often communicated to the president by a letter signed by the chair of the board.

Some boards indicate that this review is an opportunity to provide guidance to the president in relation to time management issues. For example, the letter from the chair to the president might indicate that the president should spend "as much as sixty percent" of the president's schedule in fundraising. On the other hand, one president reports that such a letter defined, permitted, and advised the president to "follow through on regular time in rest and *re-charging batteries* away from the job."

One school has developed a more elaborate presidential review process that is implemented every four to five years to determine how well the skills of the president match the skills needed for the tasks that will move the seminary forward over the next five years. This president reports that he takes such an assessment very seriously, as he must ask himself if he has (or can acquire) the needed skills for what is clearly an evolving job. He reports that contracts detailing these conversations are very helpful to him, and, as a result of such assessment, both he and the board now better understand his role as president.

Still other boards determine that every five years they will conduct a more "in-depth review" of both president and board leadership than what they do on an annual basis. This review often is reported as involving the hiring of persons who visit the campus, hold extensive interviews, and then write a report, while also making oral suggestions directly to both the board and the president. This five-year review is part of a contractual obligation on the part of both the president and the board, as is each annual review.

Administrative staff assessment

The president is also the person who sees to it that all administrative staff have current job descriptions, an annual review of performance in their positions, and written follow-through resulting in a letter detailing concerns, accolades, and future priorities for work.

Almost every school has an administration manual in place that details how such administrative staff assessment will occur. Many schools develop their own template. The supervisor (often the dean or president) fills out the template and then gives it to the administrator. That person writes a response or simply affirms that they are in agreement with what has been written. Both parties spend sufficient time discussing what has been written so that both are willing to sign the resulting document. This paper is then placed in the administrator's confidential employment file.

Most schools note that administrator assessment occurs before the end of the fiscal year and, in some cases, also note that stellar performance is reflected in the determination of individual salary increases. Other schools, where salaries are increased by a percentage "across the board," still find such assessment procedures to be useful in keeping the institution "on track." In other words, "performance audits" (as one dean names these) can be used both in building "a paper trail" that can justify the dismissal of a specific employee whose performance is not up to par and, more positively, as several presidents have noted, can "unearth new systemic possibilities" and "open up substantial individual issues that could have remained un-discussed, but were surfaced through this process."

Policy manuals and legalities

Accrediting visitors begin their visit on a campus in the office of the president. They will ask the president about the relevance of the school's mission statement and how it is used in planning initiatives and assessment procedures. They will, then, visit other administrators. At some point in those conversations, each administrator will be asked about annual reviews and how they understand that process. At lunch with members of the governing board that same day, another committee member will ask how the board conducts a review of itself and its members, and how (and in what way) they review their president.

These questions, while blunt, are to be expected. So, too, are concerns about manuals for each administrative area. Such manuals detail procedures for hiring, student dismissal, what can be expected when tuition bills are due, when tenure is not granted, or when charges of sexual harassment are leveled at a staff member. Manuals often are not on the assessment guru's screen, but schools that have been challenged in court about any of the above issues will attest that following a well-written procedure in a current manual has saved them significant pain and grief.

Manuals need to be assessed on a regular basis by those who must live by them and by those who have expertise in each particular policy area and in the general area of labor law. The composition, for example, of an adequate institutional sexual harassment policy is not an easy thing. The president can appoint a task force, but they will quickly discover that deciding what should be in print and what should be left out are difficult issues. Some task force members will inevitably draft language that is too specific; others will favor a juridical style that might result in all charges being treated with equal legitimacy. A consultant, skilled at walking persons through a series of role plays regarding a particular policy that appears in a manual, can help reveal, for instance, how "step three" of the policy does not coherently follow "step two."

Nevertheless, let's assume that a sexual harassment policy is crafted, and subsequently hearings among various constituencies are held. After this, the rewritten policy is approved by the appropriate governance structures, and the policy is printed in all of the relevant manuals. Assessment, in this case, can only really occur when an actual case is raised. Then, the lawyers will get involved. Perhaps they read drafts of the policy as it was being created,

60

but no matter—they will note that no policy in a manual is ever fully understood until a "real" case occurs. It is only under such circumstances that glaring omissions can be seen. The lawyers will suggest that the school hold all policy changes until after this case is settled. That is, once a case is being decided, the best advice is to follow the procedures exactly as they are printed in the appropriate manual. Later, there will be opportunity to discuss how the policy worked and how it might be improved.

The mission statement

A school's mission statement articulates those things a school believes it is called to do, and should function in a way that helps the school say "yes" or "no" to the numerous possible strategies that always emerge in assessment. Dialogue about how any proposed institutional initiative is, or is not, related to the mission statement should be lively and decisive before any action is taken. In this manner, the mission statement guides the institution in its comprehensive institutional planning process.

In many schools, the president offers a yearly reflection to the governing board as to how well the institution has, or has not, followed its mission statement in all its endeavors. It is crucial that such conversation be held regularly and that adequate time is set aside to do it thoroughly. It is appropriate to place such a conversation on the agenda for a governing board meeting near the end of either the academic or fiscal year.

If and when the governing board determines that the school and its circumstances/constituencies have changed so significantly that it is time to rework the mission statement, a drafting committee (with a purposive composition) can produce a paper to be initially discussed and vetted by the governing board and then distributed for comment to the school's constituencies. If appropriate, regional hearings involving outside stakeholders can also be held. Input is received by the drafting committee and discussions on the draft occur within the board. After sufficient time, a "final" draft is produced. It is, again, distributed to constituencies. And, after receiving and processing all relevant responses, the new statement is, then, voted upon at a regularly scheduled meeting of the board. The newly approved mission statement would, then, be distributed to appropriate persons and institutions while plans are made for its salient themes to be broadcast on everything from academic program learning objectives to car bumper stickers and baseball caps! Academic programs will need to be adjusted to incorporate the emphases of the new statement. It should appear in the school's catalog and on recruitment materials; and, the school moves forward.

Something like this scenario unfolds in numerous schools because the president and the board understand the importance of a clearly understood and relevant institutional mission statement. It is, however, the president who keeps the school's mission statement uppermost in the minds of most board members. For example, one ATS school president includes the mission statement as a reading in the fall convocation; another president has the governing board read the school's mission statement before they discuss and approve their proposed budget. The mission statement is both the authoritative document that defines the principles of assessment in every other aspect of the school's life, and itself needs regularly, if not frequently, to be assessed if a school would, on the one hand, be enabled to focus on what it does particularly well, and, on the other, respond to shifts in contextual factors, both internal and external.

Board member assessment

It is clear that both the president and the governing board are the primary actors in any assessment of the school's mission statement, but such assessment of the mission statement often is accompanied by other assessment procedures, including assessment of the governing board as a whole and assessment of the members of the governing board. To the degree that regular assessment of the board, its members, and the school's mission occurs, the board acts as a model for the rest of the school. It is a certainty, for instance, that it is hard to convince an institution to begin a serious assessment plan until or unless such assessment includes the board and its members.

What might board member assessment look like? The most frequently described format for board member assessment suggests that a board development committee should be charged with the annual review of each member on the basis of a carefully designed self-assessment questionnaire completed by each trustee. Because this committee identifies and recruits new board members, orients and educates them to board responsibilities, and monitors their engagement in board activities and responsibilities, it is an appropriate body to conduct board member assessment. A self-assessment questionnaire report also provides a way for board members to make a graceful exit when they are no longer effectively engaged. Term appointments with clear renewal policies constitute another strategy to maintain healthy and active boards. Those who no longer can, or no longer desire, to fulfill the responsibility of a regular member of the board can join auxiliary advisory groups or committees, designed to provide less demanding ways for friends of the institution to support the school. In any case, assessing board structures and board members is made doubly difficult when board members have life terms—this should be avoided where possible.

What we have learned

Accreditors are concerned, fundamentally, with the health of the institution. Accreditors emphasize institutional planning and assessment not because they harbor an authoritarian agenda, but because institutional planning and assessment matter. A clear policy manual detailing well-thought-out procedures matters. Good job descriptions and annual reviews make a difference in how work is done within a school. Institutional self-understanding, in light of a clearly crafted mission statement, is particularly important—as is the way a governing board monitors its own performance in light of that mission statement.

A good board will recognize that it must hold itself accountable for its overall performance and the effectiveness of its own procedures. Regular assessment of the school's mission statement, individual board member performance, and the effectiveness of the general board serves a crucial function in creating an intentional process of self-correction as the board leads the school to fulfill its mission.

CHAPTER 6

ASSESSMENT AND STRATEGIC PLANNING

"When you have assembled what you call your 'facts'
in logical order, it is like an oil-lamp
you have fashioned, filled, and trimmed;
but which will shed no light
unless first you light it."

Saint-Exupéry[14]

The days of the "great five-year strategic plan" are long gone. At the same time, flexible, assessment-based strategic planning has become, in the words of one seminary president, "the most crucial aspect of what a good president does today in theological education." This chapter considers the president's role in building a (good) strategic planning process anchored by assessment.

Institutional assessment and *strategic planning* form two interwoven strands. It could be argued that it does not matter so much what specific process of assessment or planning is being used by a school, but it matters very much in both instances that the president put in place and attend to interpretive locations where both processes are made to intersect with disciplined regularity.

Conducting the process

In relation to both strategic planning and institutional assessment, the president conducts the process; that is, the president is the band leader and not a solo instrumentalist. While analogies always break down, institutional assessment is very much like the daily or weekly rehearsal of an orchestra. As conductor, the president rehearses the various elements of the school's music that are congruent with the school's mission. In this process, the conductor works with the strings, percussion, and brass sections as needed. The president also praises, cajoles, and helps the "instrumentalists" do their best as they rehearse together, working patiently through the difficult parts of the composition and combining all the sections.

In rehearsal there are passages that are played, reworked, and then played again. Line by line, music emerges but there are false starts and occasional breakdowns while things can only be described as chaotic. Still, at the end of the day, all the tiny steps made in rehearsal are understood by both the members of the orchestra and the conductor to have worked together in making a significant difference in the music that will later be performed in "orchestra hall."

The scope and degree of this work

Presidents note that the difference between institutional assessment and strategic planning is one of scope and degree, that is, both follow a similar process, but **institutional assessment** involves shepherding regular (even constant) reflection on each of the day-in, day-out activities at all levels of the school's life, while **strategic planning** involves assessing key indicators with the underlying intent of moving a school through potentially historic changes. Following our analogy, institutional assessment is like the orchestra's rehearsal, while strategic planning is more like the orchestra's major performance. Tiny steps leading to incremental change typify the institutional assessment process; more sizeable steps must be contemplated and intentionally placed on the table in the strategic planning process.

An example of on-going institutional assessment: the budget cycle

Accordingly, on-going institutional assessment in most schools follows a fairly arbitrary cyclical calendar determined and occasionally re-calibrated by experience. For example, the budget process always follows a more or less predictable annual cycle, demanding data input in the fall from all of the school's divisions, and arriving via the president's council in a spring document that, once again, demarcates how a particular school will implement its educational mission in the upcoming fiscal year.

In this regard, one school regularly sets aside half the time spent in its council/cabinet meetings during October through May for dealing with budgetary concerns. Monthly actuals are always examined. With computer access, the CFO daily monitors budget activity and provides council members with percentages spent plus how those percentages fit the school's budgetary data. Questions of financial concern are generated; discussion involves all officers.

The president keeps track of various data gathering initiatives connected to several key indicators peculiarly important to this school. The *dashboard* format suggested in Chapter Five is employed. The president believes that while the council's interpretation of such data can generate useful proposals, these should be formally considered only after the CFO runs several financial models. Such scenarios are employed by the CFO and the president in order "to capture certain windows of opportunity," as the president puts it.

The data collected and the several alternative financial models generated, the council can proceed to build the new budget. As budgets involve not so much abstract numbers but people's jobs, the number and quality of employee benefits, and anxieties about personal and institutional futures, nurturing trust is crucial. Transparency is the best means of creating and maintaining trust as all involved can see the actual situation and work together to ensure that resources are shared as equitably as possible, while being allocated in ways that help fulfill the school's mission.

In the school mentioned above, the CFO has put together a "red-flag" calendar with some thirty key moments identified. A "Budget Code Book" details the particulars of each budgetary line item. If adjustments to the budget need to occur, the CFO works with each department to identify which unspent lines can be re-allocated. By May of each year a balanced budget, using less than 5% draw on seminary endowment, has been created and approved. By the following October, the previous year's audited financial report and management letter is back on the council's desk; once again the budgetary process begins.

Critical reflection on the process

In the above example, there is no guarantee that the council's attentiveness to the yearly budgetary process will result in a better institution, but schools that do not pay such close attention to budgetary matters regularly find themselves in financial trouble. A thoughtful, on-going appraisal of transparent data can encourage a school to make the necessary mid-stream adjustments in terms either of increasing revenues or cutting expenses in order to live within its means.

Asking good questions and making realistic proposals based on good data also clarifies unrealistic assumptions about the budget's relationship to the mission of the school. All schools have implicit understandings regarding what "really" matters. But the budget tells someone who is an outsider, explicitly, what "really" counts. Making such implicit assumptions explicit involves institutional assessment procedures for all personnel and all program units. Not only does an institution need carefully crafted job descriptions for each position and procedures for the regular review of every employee in every department, but it needs regularly to ask and answer serious questions about the nature of the school. For instance, a question such as:

"what number and kind of faculty, what number and kind of students, and what number and kind of physical resources are needed for us to remain viable and fulfill our mission?"

can only be answered realistically in relation to various strategic indicators, such as the size of the pool of potential applicants, the cost of educating each student, the fundraising cost per dollar raised, the current endowment draw-down, and the monthly net operating profit and loss figures.

Data uncovered by such work on the budget, when set beside the institution's mission plan, will also uncover those agendas and assumptions that might have once worked but may no longer work (or no longer be missionally appropriate).

In the above example of one school's budget-making process, we have no access to detailed data, but we can imagine that disciplined attention to such data will provide the key administrators at that council with information about possible trajectories that, over time, will lead them to make necessary adjustments to that budget. The president is the critical player in this process of uncovering such assumptions about trajectories and "naming" that which "we" might "become."

Once this school's budgetary numbers are in place for the new financial year, the institutional assessment process will continue to pose new questions that will help to shape the next budget process. New evaluative data will be sought as to the appropriateness of both the amounts allocated in the current year and the various lines to which the allocations were made. This is the daily work of *institutional assessment*. As such, it provides key information for the assessment loop, keeps the "shop" moving in the right direction, and prepares all those on board to consider if any radical adjustments might be needed. Such radical adjustments would be determined by the larger process of strategic planning.

Why strategic planning?

There are many reasons why an institution engages in strategic planning. The office of the president may be in the midst of major leadership transitions, and the new players are seeking a more complete and coherent picture of the institution. Or, the ten year re-assessment accreditation visit has unearthed, through the self-study process, several trajectories that are either deeply troubling or exciting to the governing board. Or, perhaps one of the accrediting agencies has pointed out a set of critical issues that must be addressed, and, in conversations about these issues, new missional objectives that could re-position the school in a new and very different direction emerge. Or, a set of unexpected factors comes to light, which, in a surprising way, seem to be pulling the school back to its roots, but in a very unusual fashion.

Frankly, more is at stake when strategic long term planning initiatives are being explored by the institution than one might think. A poorly chosen initiative can prove costly, and "strategic" moves must rely upon more than intuitive hunches.

Theological schools also must adjust to complexities that arrive, unbidden, on their doorsteps. A major gift is received and a chair is endowed. But, the next day, a fire destroys the main administration building. Neither event can be controlled. Both must be responded to in line with missional objectives. Such disorienting events are fairly rare, however. More regularly, schools find themselves trying to understand the potential trajectories of everyday, mundane decisions, which may seem unimportant now but can result in major shifts in direction over the long term. Regular institutional assessment provides a school with a set of useful practices to make good decisions on a regular basis—and to face a crisis. But, on occasion, a school needs to wrestle with the "big picture" more intentionally. Hence, the need for strategic planning.

An example of strategic planning: moving a school

Strategic initiatives rely on good administrators who are willing to face major issues and not run from them. "Plans" come to life through people. And strategic planning usually involves more than just the interior team. Key persons, coupled with God's grace, often embody more than what was initially hoped for when a strategic team is assembled.

For example, a landlocked seminary with a growing student population asked its team of seminary executives to consider options for the future of the school. All chimed in with proposals, a number of which seemed reasonable and realistic. What route to take?

The issues were clear: more (and better) space was needed; current buildings were in need of repair; and asbestos removal would be involved. The seminary was located in an increasingly affluent area, and numerous "home developers" were hoping for the possible sale of the school. The constituencies served wanted more convenient access to the school and its program, and land near a transportation link was (possibly) available.

The assessment questions were many.
• Will a move harm or help our mission?
• Will our constituents give sufficient resources for us to make this move realistic?
• What would be the actual amount of money realized by the sale?
• What would a new campus need to look like to deliver good theological education into the next century?

Gathering the necessary data from all of the different contexts was difficult. The development officer needed to check with the school's constituents and keep key persons regularly informed as to progress. The CFO was busy with architects, banks, and funding proposals. Numerous scenarios had to be run through the school's financial modeling process. The academic dean had to name what a "good" educational building should look like and had to do this quickly. The president seemed constantly on the phone or computer or out of the office, meeting with all manner of persons who thought that they had the land that would meet all seminary criteria.

Several potential resolutions collapsed for one reason or another, but then one day things came together and stayed together. A decision was reached, contracts were signed, and deadlines were announced.

And everyone seemed happy.

The real work, however, was yet to come, as the president's council began to recognize how this initiative might result in still other initiatives. For example, the work begun by the council had transformed the governing board. That board had come through with financial, emotional, and intellectual resources. Several board members had stepped forward; the board now understood its mission in a much deeper and richer way, and it now understood that it would have to continue to play a major role in the future of the seminary.

Looking back, the president noted that this move could only have occurred because of team effort, and that the "team" eventually included numerous persons both inside and outside the school.

The president was fond of remembering the biblical story of Moses, who initially did all the work himself. Jethro, Moses's father-in-law, told Moses that his trying to adjudicate all the problems of Israel by himself was not helpful. Jethro told Moses that he needed to appoint others to share in the work that Moses was doing by himself. After dispersing the load, Jethro said, "Now all the people will go to their tents in peace." "And," said the president (with a twinkle in his eye), "Moses won't burnout!!"

Critical reflection

In this example, a competent president and a solid administrative team grappled with the implications of sometimes conflicting data. While the four-point assessment "loop" discussed in Chapter Two is not overtly visible, that loop's initial step of questioning the school's viability in its immediate context is clearly evident: "Is it better for us to strip asbestos from this aging and not very useful set of buildings, or should we sell this valuable land and relocate elsewhere?" Such questioning, articulated by the president, became a hot topic with faculty, the board, and various constituencies supportive of the seminary. These conversations led to the formation of a broad-based set of strategic initiative committees charged with gathering appropriate and useful data (step number two in the assessment loop). While steps one and two clearly overlapped, caution was emphasized about not "jumping to conclusions too early."

Step number two (data gathering) was laden with its own hermeneutic of suspicion. For example: "Were the track records of some of the potential brokers who eagerly courted the school a matter of public record?" Due diligence in this terrain was a continuing concern for both the president and some of the board's business members who advised extreme caution at taking some of the scenarios that various brokers presented at face value.

In contrast, the faculty actually seemed to enjoy the opportunity to determine with the academic dean "what a good educational facility for theological educators" should look like.

Most of what occurred in the school's earliest steps followed those ideas on interior audit-taking noted in Chapter Four. Given those processes, every committee accordingly produced a lot of data, some of it dubious in nature, but much of it useful for constructing a set of alternative proposals.

Step three (interpretation of data as proposals are generated) was at times both exhilarating and frustrating. Key players and assorted trusted consultants and constituency focus groups engaged in what the president called "an ongoing conversation." When a set of discrete proposals actually emerged from this conversation, the president asked the CFO to "crunch the numbers." Such financial modeling had a sobering effect on the discussion, but suddenly what had appeared as numerous possibilities were pragmatically reduced to one or two realistic ones.

An ongoing conversation

Throughout these initial steps the president's enthusiasm about the process was remarkably infectious. It spread and grew as the president met with faculty, administrators, and various constituency representatives almost on a daily basis, extolling the wide range of options facing the school. Formal "communication letters" and a wide use of e-mail and the telephone led to numerous constituency gatherings where "talking out loud" seemed to help further clarify the school's future direction. "We kept talking about the school's mission," said the president, "and I was, at times, overly enthusiastic about a possible move and, at other times, terrified by how a misstep could lead to disaster. I prayed a lot, and I asked a lot of people to join with us in such prayer."

Much of what occurred in this phase can be understood as the result of the exterior audit process recommended in Chapter Four. This hectic period of proposal-making and ongoing interpretation led to several of what had once seemed viable proposals being dropped, but a critical moment took place late in this process as the governing board announced that a decision had been reached and the school would move. The particulars were yet to be determined, but marching orders had now been issued.

In one sense, this move was the beginning of step four. Step four (reaching a decision and determining the strategy and tactics necessary for implementing that decision) took still more work, but unanimity was the watchword in this process. The decision to sell and move was met with prayers of thanksgiving; what was yet to be resolved were the sticky particulars. At this juncture, the president noted, "we've been blessed by a good process that brought us together. We could have fragmented into disunity at any number of moments, but God's grace is such that we did not. I think one large plot of land we are now considering will become our next 'home,' but that's only a step. We don't relocate campuses as our mission. Our mission is to educate folks for the church, so this initiative has to be understood as something that enables us to do just that."

Strategic planning takes a school into unexplored terrain where experience from *institutional assessment* helps, but doesn't provide all that will be needed, particularly because the school (might) move onto new (unmapped) terrain. But *strategic planning* can also result in major changes without physical relocation. Such deliberate change is the core of the case that follows.

An example from the past: a seminary forms ministers

It is clear that seminary presidents and key administrators have for many years sorted through conflicting data that suddenly appeared at their schools. They never called what they were doing "assessment," but they went about their business with care and thoughtfulness. Eventually, institutional observers and key players began to systematize what was being done, and, subsequently, accrediting agencies started to expect schools to have in place institutional assessment plans.

Accordingly, we can look back into every school's history and discover examples of the thoughtful interweaving of institutional assessment and institutional strategic planning. In many cases, both interior and exterior audits actually occurred, and schools were clear-eyed regarding the dangers that could impede the forward progress of their schools. Indeed, faithful leaders in a previous age sometimes risked institutional viability even as they hewed to their missional understandings. For example, when the author of this book joined a seminary faculty, he was made aware of the history of that school. Part of that verbalized narrative noted how important it had been in an earlier moment of the school's history when it had relocated into the middle of "a world-class university." Strong, federated ties had been forged with this university.

Apparently, at first, the seminary enjoyed its federated status that tied it to the university. The two schools formed this relationship with good will, and for more than a decade the relationship prospered. One day, however, in a conversation with the seminary president, the university president suggested that if an entering seminarian was "good enough to pass every senior exam in the initial month of school, that person should immediately graduate." The president of the seminary allowed that "becoming an effective minister took more than the ability to pass tests."

This argument spilled over into faculty conversations. A careful check of interior and exterior constituencies indicated strong feeling on this issue. The university hewed more to a content-driven understanding. The crucial consideration on the part of the seminary appeared to be concern for adequate *formation* of ministers.

In open hearings the seminary faculty argued that adequate formation for ministry meant, among other things, supervision, mentoring, and work in areas that weren't easily graded—like spirituality and personal character. They strongly believed that a certain amount of time spent in structured reflection on the practice of ministry was also a necessary element for such education.

The university faculty disagreed; if the new student could pass academic senior exams, that student should graduate.

The disagreement continued to deepen. The seminary faculty came to see more and more clearly that its mission was to be engaged in the formation of ministers, that this was what it meant to be a seminary. It also became clearer and clearer that to fulfill this mission it would be necessary to withdraw from the seminary's very close affiliation with the university. And the seminary did exactly that, withdrawing and standing alone as an unfederated institution.

Critical reflection: where's the loop?

While no formal assessment "loop" was employed by the seminary in contemplating this radical change in trajectory, it is clear in reading the school's history that the four steps were engaged in some form. First, intense questioning occurred: "What will the university demand and can we live with it?" This led to a collection of relevant data (step two). Constituencies were informed because their understandings were deemed important. Seminary faculty met formally and informally in order to weigh the various costs and benefits of each possible scenario.

The president of the seminary felt that the school's best option was to pull back from the close university affiliation. This was not initially supported by the faculty, but, as data were interpreted (step three), an agreement supportive of the president was reached. They were a seminary faculty, not a university faculty. Seminary learning was something more than just an academically driven enterprise. Formation arguments were convincing; education for ministry involved the whole person and not the mind alone.

Arriving at a decision and implementing it (step four) flowed almost naturally from this process. The seminary withdrew from its "too close" affiliation with the university; today it remains an independent institution. Occasionally, a graduate from the "federated" period refers to it as the school's "golden era," but new students continue to applaud the seminary curriculum, perhaps confirming the decision to break those ties. And, they still benefit from geographic proximity to the university with access to resources such as health care facilities, libraries, and the field house. Meanwhile, the seminary continues to pursue its mission, committed still to the idea that readiness for ministry entails something more than just the ability to pass exams.

What we have learned

While historic decisions, such as moving a school or reconfiguring long-standing institutional affiliations, should be made as the result of careful *strategic planning*, regular and on-going *institutional assessment* more often results in smaller alterations, like reshaping specific budget priorities. At the same time, a dozen such alterations in the budget can be said to make a major difference in how the school fulfills, or does not fulfill, it's mission.

This means that not all new data will result in radical change, but *institutional assessment* may well be the process of putting into place small changes that will keep the institution not only in touch with itself, but also with the changing conditions that threaten its viability. While the budget isn't the only place this argument works, it serves as a good example of how small decisions, systematically connected, add up to measurable sums of consequence for the mission of the institution.

Nevertheless, a president cannot fully control a school's future even with the best assessment/planning process in place—and that is where a deeper sense of risk connecting mission and vocation move *institutional assessment* into *strategic planning*. The examples of major decisions such as moving a seminary campus and redefining "what counts" as learning suggest the crucial nature of those steps that were taken. Both choices altered each school's sense of itself; these were big steps, not lightly taken. In both instances, the president and governing board recognized which key indicators should be determinative and asked the right questions, building on competent institutional assessment procedures and, thereby, tethering a strategic planning process to reality.

In other words, every president faces decisions, both large and small, that can reshape a school for better or for worse—and yet which simply must be faced and decided. Thoughtful presidents have come to recognize that flexible, assessment-based strategic planning is "the most critical aspect of what a good president does today."

Conclusion

Chapter one introduced the image of a four-step assessment "loop" and suggested that such processes be implemented in theological schools, while noting that a "loop" should be used evocatively rather than prescriptively. Chapters two through five suggested how "closing" such "loops" could be helpful as a theological school worked with, respectively, students, degree programs, and various institutional departments. Finally, in this sixth chapter, I have suggested that the daily work of closing the various loops of assessment is the best way, over the long haul, to build an assessment culture that leads organically to useful strategic planning. The ideas expressed throughout these several, later chapters were also meant to be evocative and not prescriptive. Each school has to create and close the several assessment "loops" most appropriate to its mission and context. It is this author's hope, in any case, that the personal and communal discernment processes contained within these chapters will nurture healthy, on-going self-evaluation in theological schools.

"At our most insecure,
  we want to materialize and quantify the holy
  so we can keep an eye on it."

Daniel Taylor[15]

When I was in college, I intended to become a high-school teacher. One step on that journey was a year of supervised teaching in a public school. In order to get from my college to the school, I needed transportation. My mom and dad agreed to help me, and we began to look for a second-hand car. Eventually we purchased one that showed a lot of wear, but still "had a few good miles left to run." Before we bought it, the car was examined by our neighborhood mechanic and pronounced to be in good health. The mechanic and my dad carefully introduced me to the system that I now owned. Both men let me know that it was now my responsibility to keep the car running well, and that a routine check (if done regularly and with care) would alert me to any budding difficulties. They both assured me that I was competent enough to maintain this particular car.

I repaid their trust in me. Apart from a couple of scary moments—one having to do with cheap tires and another with a rotten radiator hose—that car ran as well (or better) than almost any car I've owned since. The man who bought it from me (for the same amount that my dad and I paid for it) subsequently drove it from Pennsylvania to Los Angeles and back without incident. While I doubt that he is still driving that car, I believe that he must also have paid close attention to what our friendly mechanic and my dad called the automotive system, with equally positive results.

This book is intended to introduce you to a very different sort of system, that of assessment. Still, the advice given me concerning the maintenance of my first car seems important to emphasize here. Assessment is all about regular check-ups to help the whole institution run well and stay healthy. Such is the purpose behind all the component parts that make up an assessment system, which we have been discussing.

Perhaps a caution is in order. While I like my analogy, equating the maintenance of a used car to assessment in a theological school errs at several points. First, the car is a machine, and I am wary of mechanistic assessment models. While one can perhaps forgive a former academic dean for desiring to create a well-oiled system of assessment procedures that simply run on its own, that kind of administrator's dream could easily become a nightmare. First, theological schools are not machines; they are complex communities that thrive (or fail to) based not only on the quality of scholarship pursued but also on the quality of relationship cultivated. Assessment in this context must be disciplined but it also must be flexible and compassionate. Second, machines break down, wear out, and have planned obsolescence built into them. No one who has experienced any of these conditions would want to visit them upon folk who educate or are being educated in a theological institution. Nevertheless, while a school that works at self-assessment may fail and close, such tragic results are not inevitable and the continual self-corrections made possible because of good assessment procedures are the best way I know to ensure a long and healthy future for any institution.

An image that strikes me as being better than that of a car is a community of caring humans collectively engaged in the disciplined practice of assessment as discernment. Such is, after all, what theological educators ought to be about. I remember, as a junior faculty member, sitting in the faculty assembly as we commented on each new student following a week of orientation and retreat. One new student's name provoked several negative comments as to whether or not that student was equipped to be "in seminary." Uncomfortable with the haste of this judgment, a senior faculty member spoke up. He suggested that we, as a collective faculty, would have "numerous occasions this fall to connect with this student," and "it would be well were we to see this person from a variety of angles before we decide what ought to be done." This was sage advice from someone who noted that he "often was surprised at how an initial glimpse cannot tally the whole soul." He also noted that "in human frailty as well as in grandeur we can see glimpses of the holy." Later I would remember his comments when this once-timid-and-anxious student graduated well-prepared for ministry. Assessment has to do with deep discernment; a machine cannot do this, but a community can.

Joining the faculty at the institution where I used to work required that one come to recognize this truth, that we were called to be engaged in helping individuals develop and not simply to be engaged in working with those whom we liked. This commitment got translated into a myriad of little, homely acts. For example, most of this school's procedures began with the word "normally." "Normally the candidate will . . ." On more than one occasion, I witnessed caring faculty bend what appeared to be rigid degree requirements in order to help facilitate a good student's learning trajectory. Unlike machines, communities (even academic communities) need the flexibility that comes with using words like "normally." However, such flexibility cannot mean that "anything goes" either. Instead, it requires constant, interpretive judgments, a kind of atmosphere of discernment that is embodied responsibly in daily decisions that move the community forward in realistic hope.

And, now, from a distance, I am also beginning to recognize that even such a gathering of faculty—at a certain time, on a certain day, once in every term—necessitated a kind of "system," a machine, if you will, that regularly worked! Perhaps, given that I still consider myself an administrator and so like its helpfulness in emphasizing the importance of regular attention to keep things running smoothly, I'll hold onto the car illustration. But, after these last reflections, I'll tack on Daniel Taylor's words that serve as the epigraph above as a reminder of what is, after all, most important.

In other words, check the tires, the radiator hoses, and your map—creating and utilizing a variety of assessment "loops" to help you discern which way to go—but don't make it more important than the people and the mission that it is meant to serve, don't make it a box to contain the holy. And then as you put your car in gear for the next leg of your journey—ensuring that your "loops" are closed and work to foster self-correction—pay attention—mindfully and prayerfully—to the ways all these things interconnect in human terms, and the system, God willing, may just take you where you could not otherwise go.

NOTES

1. From Conan Doyle, *Scandal in Bohemia*, quoted in Colin Dexter, *Death is Now My Neighbor* (London: Mac-Millan, 1996), 107. Original source: Conan Doyle, *Scandal in Bohemia* in *The Adventures of Sherlock Holmes* in *The Complete Sherlock Holmes* (New York: Doubleday, 1930), 163.

2. Anonymous source quoted in Gretchen E. Ziengenhals, "Faculty Life and Seminary Culture: It's about time and money" in Malcolm L. Warford (editor), *Practical Wisdom: On theological teaching and learning* (New York: Peter Lang, 2004), 52.

3. As a part of this process, more than half of ATS schools use *Profiles of Ministry: An Assessment Program Designed for the Seminary Student*. It assesses individuals with a wide range of ministry-related characteristics and is available through ATS.

4. Maria Tatar, "The short list: resistance to 'interdisciplinarity'" in *The Chronicle of Higher Education* 51:19 (14 January 2005), B2.

5. Eileen Campbell-Reed in a paper presented at a consultation on Ph.D. education at the Wabash Center, Fall 2004.

6. Patricia Dutcher-Walls, "Prelude to Curricular Revision: Learning Assessment, and Competence in Ministry," in *Ten Cases of Curricular Revision* (The Association of Theological Schools, 2003).

7. For those interested in deeper exploration of integrated learning, see Mary Taylor Huber and Pat Hutchings, *Integrative Learning: Mapping the terrain* (Washington: The Carnegie Foundation for the Advancement of Teaching and The Association of American Colleges and Universities, 2004).

8. A composite based on two advertisements for chief executive officers in *The Chronicle of Higher Education* 52:6 (30 September 2005), C80-81.

9. Gordon T. Smith, "Attending to the collective vocation" in L. Gregory Jones and Stephanie Pausell (editors), *The Scope of Our Art: The Vocation of the Theological Teacher* (Grand Rapids: Eerdmanns, 2002), 250.

10. Robert Cooley, "Understanding a Seminary's Culture, Context, and Change: A Model for Strategic Assessment and Planning." An unpublished talk delivered at *The ATS Presidential Intensive Week*, Sante Fe, New Mexico, December, 2004.

11. For example, every two years individual ATS schools receive comparative data as to how they stand relative to all other ATS schools. This information arrives in a *Strategic Information Report*; the single school can then request comparative data with an additional five to fifteen other schools (IPPR) for a small fee.

12. "Dashboards" was a plenary presentation by Rebekah Bassinger at *The ATS Presidential Intensive Week*, Santa Fe, New Mexico, December 2004. The four-part example is the product of presidential work groups at that event.

13. *In Trust* offers a board self-assessment package, including a sample survey page and pricing information at www.intrust.org/resource; scheduling the package for your school can occur via the toll-free number (877-234-3895) or at crklein@intrust.org.

14. From Saint Exupéry, *The Wisdom of the Sands*, quoted in Colin Dexter, *Death is Now My Neighbor* (London: MacMillan, 1996), 146.

15. Daniel Taylor, *In Search of Sacred Places: Looking for Wisdom on Celtic Holy Islands* (Saint Paul, Minnesota: Bog Walk Press, 2005).